Compassion-Driven Innovation

GutterTex is amazing!
Thanks you so much
for being ahead of the
curve and for the
honor of sharing your
story.

Nicole Pinedo

Compassion-Driven Innovation

12 Steps for Breakthrough Success

Nicole Reineke, Debra Slapak,
and Hanna Yehuda

BUSINESS EXPERT PRESS

Leader in applied, concise business books

First published in 2022 by
Business Expert Press, LLC
222 East 46th Street, New York, NY 10017
www.businessexpertpress.com

ISBN-13: 978-1-63742-161-1 (paperback)
ISBN-13: 978-1-63742-162-8 (e-book)

Business Expert Press Service Systems and Innovations in Business and Society Collection

Collection ISSN: 2326-2664 (print)
Collection ISSN: 2326-2699 (electronic)

First edition: 2022

10 9 8 7 6 5 4 3 2 1

We dedicate this book to our families, who have shaped our understanding of compassion and helped us to feel and practice it every day.

From Nicole: To Gerhard, Alex, Lydia, Roger, and Roseanne—the whole of my heart, with whom all things are an adventure. To my family by blood and marriage, and my friends who have supported me through thick and thin for decades—you make life meaningful. I am forever grateful to you all.

From Debra: To my husband, Joe, who remembers to light a candle. To my daughter, Grace, who casts out the shadows and gives the vulnerable a voice. To my mom and dad, Opal and Aubrey Harper, who showed me that everything is possible. And to you who chose me to be your family regardless of DNA, thank you for your enduring love.

From Hanna: To the loves of my life: Roy, who always believed I would fulfill my dreams and Amit, Noam, and Eden, who are my reasons for being. To my parents, siblings, and family, you are forever in my heart at all times. And to my inspiring teacher Thich Nhat Hanh, and my dear friends, this is for you with gratitude and love.

Description

This book is for pathfinders—product, services, business, and nonprofit managers searching for ways to reach beyond the artificial barriers that constrain innovation and make "work" harder. Inspired by real life trailblazers and their own experiences, the authors decode the secrets of achieving breakthrough success at both organizational and interpersonal levels. Follow them as they illustrate the power of compassion united with a unique, disciplined, iterative approach to delighting customers and stakeholders. Learn to use their methodology with the help of checklists and detailed examples that will transform your thinking and skills.

Keywords

compassion; compassion-driven innovation; customer journey; buyer journey; hypothesis; innovation; invention; persona; proto-journey; proto-persona; providers; primary research; research spikes; secondary research; secondary sources; state-of-the-art; product inception; services inception; strategic methodologies; business strategy; design thinking; open innovation; agile processes; innovation methodology; invention methodology; ideation; social innovation; nonprofit innovation; ethical innovation; humane technology; social justice in business

Contents

Review Quotes

"*Pathfinders seeking to effect social change need a map to guide them along the journey. This book provides very useful advice, starting from compassion, journeying through Inclusion, Discovery, Enlightenment, and concluding with Activation and Impact. Don't leave home without it!*"—**Henry Chesbrough, Professor at UC Berkeley's Haas School of Business and author of Open Innovation**

"*The value of* Compassion-Driven Innovation *lies in its intense focus on the consumer of the innovation. I wish I had these customer-facing checklists early in my career; they would have increased the adoption rate of every invention that I ever worked on. Congratulations to the authors for summarizing decades of their experience into an easy-to-understand approach.*" —**Steve Todd, Fellow at Dell Technologies and author of *Innovate With Global Influence: Tales of High-Tech Intrapreneurs***

"Compassion-Driven Innovation *is both timely and much needed as innovators reassess meaningful work practices.*"—**Jim Spohrer, IBM Director, Cognitive OpenTech**

"*Compassion-Driven Innovation (CDI) is packed with directed problem-solving advice to advance innovations and to cultivate an effective and meaningful innovation process. An important book for every leader who wants to guide their teams to innovation success.*"—**Kathleen Moriarty, Chief Technology Officer at Center for Internet Security**

"*For business leaders and entrepreneurs looking to envision compelling innovations, this book balances both inspirational ideas and stories to motivate a new way of thinking, and a pragmatic approach and process to ensure compassion through the process.*"—**Michael Hawley, VP Experience Strategy & Research, ZeroDegrees, and Professor at Bentley University**

"Compassion-Driven Innovation is a practical guide to problem-solving that puts people first to drive to the best results—more innovation, less risk. The authors map a clearly defined methodology with a set of diverse, real-world experiences, making the concepts tangible and easy to grasp. If you're looking to unlock creativity and innovation for your business, you should pick up this book!"—**Susan Rice, Vice President of User Experience at Workiva, Inc.**

Preface

Have you ever shaken your head in frustration that your organization is doomed to mediocrity? Perhaps it is just too big or too small, too mired in tradition, or forced by circumstances to move too slowly or too quickly. These are some of the more common excuses we have heard about why organizations fail to differentiate through innovation. We respectfully disagree. We know that organizations of any size and every level of maturity can create imaginative and disruptive products and services that resonate with customers. The kind of innovation we are talking about persuades customers and other stakeholders to return again and again and even become champions for your brand.

As you and your organization become adept at delivering innovation, you have the potential to scale and influence the world in ways that stretch the bounds of imagination. You can find examples everywhere—in retail, agriculture, health care, life sciences, transportation and logistics, energy, entertainment, hospitality, and in government and nongovernment services organizations. Across every industry, those who dare to open their minds to what they *could* do to solve a problem—rather than what they *should* do based on what is incremental, easy or "next"—are the game changers.

Why Compassion Matters

We understand that you may be skeptical about the word "compassion" in the title and its use in the methodology stages. Some people may think that this is a soft or weak skill, but we implore you to keep an open mind. Until now, compassion has been the missing cornerstone in innovation paradigms.

These paradigms are not new; they have been actively explored and improved for hundreds of years. One of the most popular, design thinking, is typically credited with being documented first by Nobel Prize Laureate Herbert A. Simon in the 1960s. The original process included seven steps, where one step includes "empathy." While empathy is the recognition of others' feelings, compassion invokes a cognitive and emotional desire to help solve others' problems.

The armor of isolated empathy and dispassion that once ruled corporations (and arguably the existing approaches to innovation) no longer suffices. The world is continuously evolving. Current generations have become more aware of how corporations, organizations, and products influence the global economy, the environment, and equality. The most talented workers choose their employers based on factors such as work–life balance, ethics, and personal growth and development opportunities. Organizations and their team members can use the Compassion-Driven Innovation methodology to discover and solve challenges in ways that can benefit society and the team members responsible for generating innovation.

To succeed today, organizations and individuals must foster compassion for potential customers, for self, and for team members, especially when team members disagree. Team members must understand each others' perspectives, set egos aside and cultivate an environment in which everyone wins together. Compassion-Driven Innovation thrives in a collaborative environment.

Why You Need the Compassion-Driven Innovation Methodology

This new methodology promotes an inclusive culture that embraces the needs and input of customers and team members and the goals of their business or organization. We are sharing it to help product and services managers, technologists, engineers, and business and nonprofit leaders consistently produce and gain approval for ideas that can reshape their customers' and colleagues' experiences, while supporting corporate objectives.

Across industries and time, we have seen the struggles of those charged with delivering innovation who rely too much on what they *think* they know because they do not see an alternative. They work in isolation from other disciplines, without the skills, focus, and resources they need to establish a North Star vision and map the practical steps to delivering strategic value to their customers and other stakeholders. As a result, they risk time, money, and customer and stakeholder satisfaction and loyalty.

Compassion-Driven Innovation bridges the divide between corporate or organization strategy and solution design. Unlike previously documented methodologies, Compassion-Driven Innovation includes several steps to counter typical challenges that limit innovation. We begin the process with a theme determined by the needs of the corporation or organization that will fund the innovation. We describe how to create effective teams, fine-tune focus, establish learning as a practice, and test and challenge beliefs early, iteratively, and quickly to pivot appropriately.

By following this methodology, your team can learn to recognize and question organizational knowledge, discover challenges, prioritize solution innovation, objectively assess customer or user needs, test solutions and activate your teams to move forward confidently. Of course, no methodology is guaranteed to produce innovation, but if you follow the stages and principles of Compassion-Driven Innovation, the end result can be more innovation with less risk: risk of failing too late in the cycle, of wasting precious resources, and of damaging brand reputation or relationships in a world in which what people think about your organization's brand is a few clicks away.

An Overview of the Four Stages of Compassion-Driven Innovation

Compassion-Driven Innovation occurs in four stages: Include, Discover, Enlighten, and Activate (IDEA):

- **Include (I)** ensures that all affected disciplines are engaged in your innovation processes, and that your project aligns with your organization's objectives. Include requires compassion and respect for internal and external experts who have knowledge related to your theme. In this stage, you build an effective team, create focus, and understand state-of-the-art research, techniques, and technology from which to move forward.

- **Discover (D)** requires compassionate curiosity about the problems of buyers and users of the potential innovation. By asking the right people nonleading questions about their journeys, you can determine the challenges ripe for innovation.

- **Enlighten (E)** evokes a compassionate response to the needs and challenges you have discovered, manifesting how you can help the customer. It leads with a North Star mindset and connects your vision to current customer conditions through a phased approach that meets the priorities and resources of your organization and your customers.

- **Activate (A)** considers and addresses the needs of the extended team who will approve and build on the innovation you have illuminated. By ensuring that they have the knowledge and support to act on the vision, you help them move quickly and decisively. Your extended team will move forward together to implement the solutions or to generate high-fidelity handoffs.

We'll show you step-by-step how to implement the IDEA stages of the Compassion-Driven Innovation methodology. Out of consideration for our employers and peers, we exclude examples related to them. The examples are used with the permission of the revolutionary organizations whose names are mentioned.

As you read, we encourage you to complete the activities to reinforce what you are learning. We hope that using your organization's strategy or theme with our proven methodology will help you to identify and satisfy customer needs with unbridled innovation. We look forward to your feedback and dialogue at www.CompassionDrivenInnovation.com.

Acknowledgments

We are grateful for the contributions of the following individuals, who graciously provided their time and insights for our case studies:

- **Sivan Ya'ari, Founder and CEO of Innovation: Africa.** From the moment Sivan first saw the desperate plight of villagers in remote Africa, she has devoted her life to improving theirs. She immediately began raising funds and studying international energy management to bring essential infrastructure to villagers not slated for government relief for 15–20 more years. For the past 13 years and counting, she and her team have transformed the lives of women, men, and children across rural Africa, completing over 500 projects that sustainably deliver clean water, power, and light to nearly three million villagers in 10 countries. These projects improve access to education, food security, and refrigeration for vaccines and medications. Visit www.InnoAfrica.org for more information and to adopt a village, start a fundraiser, or donate.
- **Daniel Ouellette, Co-owner of Gutter Tex.** Daniel is a business entrepreneur who has solved homeowners' problems for over 20 years. He believes that success is built one customer interaction at a time, from the beginning to the end of each customer's journey to ensure their home is safe and beautiful. Daniel knows that his employees are his company and that homeowners want hassle-free, courteous interactions, and high-quality solutions that protect their foundations and landscaping, as well as the structure of their homes. Top ratings from customer reviews attest to his deep understanding of what his customers and employees need and his ability to deliver it. Learn more about how Gutter Tex cultivates employees and experiences that make customers happy at www.Guttertex.com.

- **Courtney Dickinson, Founder and Executive Director of Acera Education Innovation (AceraEI).** Courtney recognized 15 years ago that many children struggle to reach their full potential in the typical public school system. She imagined a world in which students' curiosity, problem-solving, and creativity are nurtured along with the science, technology, engineering, art, and math (STEAM) skills they need to thrive as adults. With a dream of igniting students' intrinsic motivation to help them reach full leadership potential, she founded the Acera School: The Massachusetts School of Science, Creativity, and Leadership. There she and her team develop and prove the value of innovative teaching techniques, which she shares with public schools through AceraEI, her outreach program. For more information or to support this cause, visit www.EI.AceraSchool.org.

Inspired by the genius of our predecessors and our contemporaries, we base our methodology on over two decades of experience with at least a dozen innovation methodologies, thinking paradigms, and processes. In addition, during the last few years, we have been fortunate to learn and grow with the help of many of our colleagues and peers, including: Deb Stokes and Robert Lincourt, whose collaboration on state-of-the-art innovation research made this book plausible. We are grateful to Jim Spohrer for believing in the promise of our methodology and the opportunity to publish this book with BEP and to our early reviewers: Henry Chesbrough, Vin Femia, Michael Hawley, Jen McGinn, Kathleen Moriarty, Roseanne Ouellette, Bill Pfeifer, Grace Gibson, Susan Rice, and Steve Todd.

Disclaimer

All logos, brands, names, trademarks, and registered trademarks are property of their respective owners. Any such instances used in this document are for identification purposes only.

Welcome to Compassion-Driven Innovation

From the time you were a small child, you have experienced compassion. Perhaps you rescued a tiny bird that fell from a nest too soon, reunited a lost pet with its humans, or encouraged a friend through a skinned knee or a bruised ego. But then you grew up and went to work, where compassion is often neglected in the race to meet deadlines and get the next big thing out the door. Worse yet, in many work cultures, compassion may be confused with *softness,* a lack of the competitive drive that pushes individuals and companies to the head of the pack. Perhaps such a culture has taught you to reserve compassion for family and friends who are ill or struggling, or for the recipients of charitable causes. If this sounds familiar, it is not surprising, but it is time for a change. The reason is simple: Denying compassion isolates us from the very people we need to help us succeed. Expressing it can inspire and empower the giver as much as the receiver.

Using Compassion to Liberate Innovation

Compassion has immense value in the business world[1]—value that spans years, careers, and lifetimes, turning strangers, customers, and colleagues into lifelong allies and friends. Consider a time when you have noticed a coworker's sacrifices, acknowledging a job well done against difficult odds. Perhaps you were moved to offer help. What did that gesture do for this person? For you? Chances are, it provided a boost to cross a finish line while making you feel like a better person. People who

---

[1] R. Hougaard, J. Carter, and N. Hobson. December 04, 2020. "Compassionate Leadership Is Necessary—but Not Sufficient." *Harvard Business Review.* htps://hbr.org/2020/12/compassionate-leadership-is-necessary-but-not-sufficient

demonstrate compassion benefit from real-time rewards, and often find that those rewards come back to them decades later. Years after helping others through a difficult time, we get a phone call in which the recipient retells a story of a kindness we have shown. We barely remember, while it changed the course of their lives.

If you feel short on compassion, do not worry. Like any other skill, you can develop it so it can take you where you want to go faster and farther. In this book, we are asking you to extend your capacity for compassion to your colleagues and customers to overcome many of the pitfalls that mire your organization in mediocrity. Compassionate collaboration with stakeholders provides diverse perspectives on the state-of-the-art and the possible. It does so by fostering a safe place to try out new ideas without fear of failure, enabling iterative leaps of understanding that lead to meaningful innovation.

We use the word *innovation* frequently throughout this book. We distinguish innovation from invention, although innovation may include invention. *Invention* is the process of creating something new, such as technologies, devices, fabrics, plants, medications, or ways of doing things. Some inventions may never connect with a customer problem in a meaningful way, and thus fail to be innovative. On the other hand, innovation is the art of applying inventions in ways that capture the hearts and minds of customers through positive change. The outcomes may range from delightful and inspirational to life changing and lifesaving. For example, a series of discoveries over the course of thousands of years led to the invention of the first solar panel in 1954. That first solar panel powered a toy Ferris wheel and a radio transmitter,[2] a delightful outcome. Decades later, solar panels are helping to deliver fresh water in areas such as Kenya.[3] Applying solar panels in new ways that solve big problems takes the original innovation to the next level.

---

[2] APS Physics. 2021. "This Month in Physics History. April 25, 1954: Bell Labs Demonstrate the First Practical Silicon Solar Cell." www.aps.org/publications/apsnews/200904/physicshistory.cfm (accessed April 24, 2021).

[3] J. Haggerty. February 06, 2020. "A New Solar Desalination System to Address Water Scarcity." *PV Magazine*. www.pv-magazine.com/2020/02/06/a-new-solar-desalination-system-to-address-water-scarcity/

Innovation isn't restricted to products or services. It can occur at any step of the buyer, influencer, or user journey. Many organizations are surprised to find that dramatic increases in adoption and revenue do not always require changing a product or service but changing how it is marketed or sold. Consider the genius of one-click purchasing: The innovation was in eliminating gates in the buyer cycle.

Why Innovation Attempts Often Fail

Attempts to innovate may fail for many reasons, but most failures originate from four sources.

Exclusivity: Assigning responsibility for innovation to a single discipline such as product managers, high-level engineers, or researchers often results in too much focus on product rather than people. Those who have deep knowledge of a product or service often work alone or in homogeneous teams to deliver the next iteration of an offering. They focus on the features and functions that they can add quickly with limited resources, while missing the big problems customers need help solving.

Failure to identify the most pressing challenges: Customer challenges can be concealed by many factors: the passage of time, changed circumstances, a lack of understanding of what is possible. Assuming what the customer needs based on experience rather than on discovery has led many teams to invent without innovating.

Overestimated value: Developing "solutions" without validating them with customers has led many teams to create a solution that is not a good fit for the priority problem(s). You may find that you are solving a downstream problem, or a lower priority problem, rather than the big one that the customer needs solved now.

Unsupported moonshots: The most striking failures of all are those that occur after innovation concepts or recommendations are identified, validated, and ready for approval. Then, to the shock of the team, the project is shelved, replaced by some less effective approach, or simply dropped altogether. You may decry such actions as organizational self-sabotage, personal vendetta, or "not-invented here" syndrome and thus unavoidable. Maybe ... or not. Our research reveals that projects that are shelved at this stage typically fail because the innovation team did not achieve alignment by:

- Ensuring consistency with the organization's strategic goals and themes;
- Creating visions that allow for levels of incremental investment;
- Convincing stakeholders of the customer-perceived value of the innovation.

Now that you know the potential stumbling blocks, we can look at how our methodology helps you avoid them.

How Our Methodology Overcomes Common Pitfalls

The Compassion-Driven Innovation methodology is the result of our experiences overcoming common obstacles to deliver innovation in multiple industries, combined with extensive research about and active practice in agile development, lean startups, design thinking, open innovation, change management, leadership and related topics. We are sharing it with you because we want you to build on what we have learned, just as we have done by leveraging the experience of those who came before us.

We have talked about what Compassion-Driven Innovation is but, practically speaking, how is it different from other innovation methods? How does it help you avoid the challenges commonly encountered in innovation projects? In addition to the overarching principle of compassion, the answer includes:

Situational awareness: The Compassion-Driven Innovation methodology includes the diverse thinking of multiple internal disciplines to establish and broaden situational awareness on which you will base initial assumptions about customer needs. We take an objective view of the current capabilities as an organization to identify and resolve skills and instill a learning process.

Agility: Compassion-Driven Innovation enables rapid pivoting and direction changes as you explore with customers and users the validity, completeness, and prioritization of your evolving assumptions about their needs and proposed solutions. We show you how to use journey maps to visualize point-in-time understanding of needs so that you can pivot to breakthrough thinking more quickly than with other methods.

Value validation: Compassion-Driven Innovation validates the value of your innovation with customers on "paper," rather than through costly prototyping, development, and implementation. We illustrate how to use storytelling and storyboarding to engage your customers in validating current and future state(s) with your solutions at their core. The authenticity and clarity of these stories will help you demonstrate the value of the innovation to other stakeholders.

Phased vision recommendations: While your innovation recommendations may be in perfect harmony with your organization's strategy, implementing them all at once may be impractical for either the customer or your organization. Compassion-Driven Innovation enables you to lead with a North Star mindset and connect your vision to current customer conditions through a phased approach that meets the priorities and resources of your organization and your customers. When you use this methodology, you can activate your preferred development and/or delivery processes without losing key innovation differentiators or delivering solutions that customers are unwilling to adopt.

Methodology Overview

The Compassion-Driven Innovation methodology enables you to:

1. Uncover customer challenges that align to your organization's themes and priorities.
2. Create stories that validate the challenges and propose solutions so that you can calibrate the outcomes with customers. These solutions are the "innovations."
3. Engage downstream stakeholders in your stories to obtain approvals to activate the innovations.
4. Prepare artifacts to guide those executing the innovations in their work of bringing the innovation to market.

The output from Compassion-Driven Innovation may be working solutions, product or services concepts, high-level design frameworks, marketing or education initiatives, workflow designs or high-fidelity implementation prototypes and plans. These outputs, and therefore the expected outcomes, are improved through iteration that advances perception and understanding based on compassion. Combined with objective (de)prioritization, this iterative approach results in creative leaps of understanding while increasing the likelihood of solving proven customer challenges in ways that align with your organization's long-term goals.

The Compassion-Driven Innovation methodology helps you create artifacts to communicate with those outside your team what the innovation is, what problems it solves, what the outcomes are expected to be, and what resources are needed to implement it.

Each stage of the methodology includes a checklist of actions to take and artifacts to create which you will use to complete your innovation or to use as inputs into your creation, development or lean process. For organizations pursuing complex innovation that may involve many departments, it may help to think of Compassion-Driven Innovation as input to your larger organizational processes, as illustrated in Figure 1.1.

We are inspired by and adapted the Fibonacci spiral to represent the methodology and show you where you are on your journey. Like

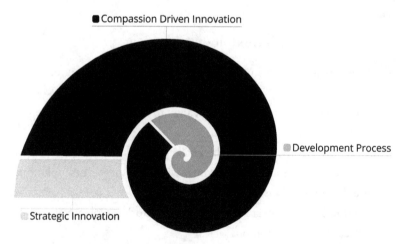

Figure 1.1 The relationship between strategic innovation, Compassion-Driven Innovation, and the development process

this spiral, we start the project with a very wide scope and possibilities bounded only by our organization's priorities. As we move through the Compassion-Driven Innovation stages and steps, we find ourselves continually honing our understanding of the challenges and possibilities, until we are ready to take a definitive step forward to activate the innovation.

Strategic innovation is an input to the Compassion-Driven Innovation methodology, and the outputs of the methodology are used to create focus within a design thinking or development process.

A secondary and enduring outcome we have experienced and observed from Compassion-Driven Innovation is its positive impact on relationships and organizational culture. The methodology honors the intent and the skills of those who are good-faith participants. It provides space for diverse perspectives and objectives so that team members can learn from each other and create exponential value together. We have felt and seen it change individuals' thoughts, feelings, and behaviors toward themselves and the larger team.

These outcomes are only possible if you bring to the methodology several foundational elements described in detail in the next section.

Foundational Elements of Compassion-Driven Innovation

To achieve innovation (or success), your team needs to bring to the process compassion for self and others, a desire to collaborate, a theme, wisdom, and time.

Compassion for Self and Others

Compassion-Driven Innovation promotes a leadership mindset. It reexamines how you are operating, not just what you are doing. Creating a safe place where ideas can flow freely without fear of judgment requires compassion for yourself, your teammates, and your customers. You will need to listen to your teammates and customers with an open mind, a willingness to see the world through the prism of their experiences and a desire to succeed together. This is not possible without embracing self-compassion. You cannot give what you do not own. You need to be ready for personal growth, reflection, and sharing bold ideas. You need to be comfortable with the idea that some of your ideas will be objectively disputed, just as you may dispute the ideas of others. You may have to embrace the team disproving or deprioritizing ideas you have become attached to, based on objective assessment. As you move through the initial steps of the methodology, you may begin to recognize, as time moves on, that what you think you understand changes, learning increases, and circumstances evolve. That may lead to the need to adjust your thoughts and actions. This does not mean you were wrong or that you have failed. It means that you have grown.

We have been practicing and iterating on this process for years, and we still find room for improvement in our methodology and in our own thoughts, beliefs, and actions. We have learned, and continually relearn, to be kind to ourselves as well as others when we recognize the need for change. That is growth.

Collaboration

It is widely accepted that the lone inventor rarely achieves breakthrough innovation. Numerous studies[4] have shown that working with collaborators improves the likelihood that invention and innovation will occur. Studies also show that collaboration which includes key stakeholders across an organization leads to higher rates of innovation and long-term organizational success.[5]

We use the word *team* to mean a group of individuals who collaborate in pursuit of a common goal. We are not suggesting that design by committee generates innovation. In fact, multiple studies show the opposite. Many challenges are complex, and solving them requires

---

[4] T.H. Chan, J. Mihm, and M. Sosa. December 31, 2019. "When Individuals are More Innovative Than Teams." *Harvard Business Review.* https://hbr.org/2019/12/when-individuals-are-more-innovative-than-teams

[5] S. Kirsner. November 29, 2019. "What Companies that Are Good at Innovation Get Right." *Harvard Business Review.* https://hbr.org/2019/11/what-companies-that-are-good-at-innovation-get-right

diverse perspectives from experts in different disciplines to spark ideas and healthy debate.

Theme

You cannot solve all the problems in the world. You must carve out a place to start changing your corner of it. You will need to focus on creating innovation in alignment with your organizational priorities. When you use the Compassion-Driven Innovation methodology with a new project, you must have an initial directive. A lot of great research is available on creating effective themes. If you are not familiar with them, just start with what you have. You may have been given a problem to solve. You may have been assigned a product to expand. You may have something as loosely defined as increasing revenue or as specific as improving the onboarding experience for a specific persona. Whatever you do, make sure that your theme sparks intrinsic motivation in your team members. When your project gets tough (and it will), you must have a goal that is truly motivating to keep the team moving forward. Regardless of the form or content for your project at hand, we will refer to this directive as your theme.

Your theme acts as a point-in-time understanding of your organizational directive. You can combine your project theme with your organization's strategic goals to set a starting point and create focus for your project.

Knowledge and Wisdom

A baseline set of knowledge and skills is a prerequisite for any team. The Compassion-Driven Innovation methodology is not designed to render an expert in veterinary medicine into a hydroponics luminary. The methodology assumes that team members will have firm baseline institutional and individual knowledge to form a situational assessment. Then you will each need to exercise wisdom to release your attachment to that knowledge and make way for deeper understanding of the situation and your ability to improve it. In the process, teams usually find that some of their assertions are flawed. You should expect this outcome and welcome it.

Time

You may be wondering how much time the methodology will take. The simple answer is that it takes 100 percent of the time you give it. Consider the size of the project you are working on and the maturity of the concept. In some cases, you may blow through a stage in a day and pivot. In other cases, you may find a gem and choose to spend weeks curating and researching.

Methodology Stages

Now that you understand the foundation on which the Compassion-Driven Innovation methodology is built, we can have a closer look at the four stages, as shown in Figure 1.2.

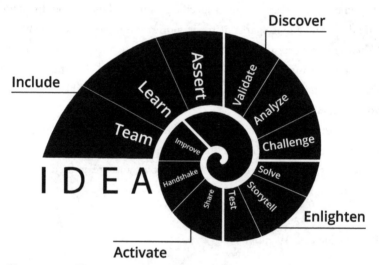

Figure 1.2 The four stages and 12 steps of the Compassion-Driven Innovation methodology

What is shown as stages and order in text is cyclical and iterative in practice. At any point in the methodology, you may learn information which makes prior assertions incomplete, a lower priority, or less true. You may discover new customer challenges that become the highest priority. This is what the methodology is designed to do.

The initial letters in the names of the four stages form an acronym: IDEA. Each of these four stages is discussed in full in the following chapters. The following is a brief overview.

- **Include (I):** In this stage, you ensure that relevant stakeholders representing distinct roles and skill sets are involved at the start of your project. You will form a cross-disciplinary team that has expertise in various aspects of the theme or project area. By showing compassion and appreciation for the knowledge of these individuals, you can quickly build an understanding of state-of-the-art from which to innovate. You will then examine your team's initial assertions.

- **Discover (D):** This stage requires curiosity about the problems of buyers and users of the potential innovation. You will start to set aside preconceived notions about what history or the status quo indicates you *should* build so that you uncover, analyze, and prioritize buyers' and users' most important problems. By asking the right people nonleading questions about their circumstances, you can determine the challenges ripe for innovation.

- **Enlighten (E):** This stage demands a compassionate response to the needs and challenges you have discovered and ends with both you and the customer becoming enlightened. You will define solutions grounded in the reality of what you *could* deliver based on resources in the desired timeframe. Next, you craft stories about how the customer's world is better because you solved their problems in the ways you have defined. Then you give them the opportunity to edit the story. Perhaps you will discover obstacles you did not discover at first or identify heroes or villains (personas) who were not mentioned previously. If you have not gotten the problems, priorities and/or the solution right, you rework the solutions and stories and share them again until you find the happy ending. By sharing with the customer stories about how their world will be better with the solution, you can calibrate your vision through rapid iteration.

- **Activate (A):** In this stage, you will consider and address the needs of internal stakeholders who will approve and build on the innovation you have illuminated. You will use compassion to understand the priorities and drivers for decision makers and the knowledge and information needs of those who will activate the solution. By ensuring each has the knowledge and support to act on the vision, you help them move quickly and decisively.

Finding issues and pivoting during Compassion-Driven Innovation sharpens your focus so that you point your investments and team toward higher value innovation. When you discover new data or challenges, you assess the priorities of what you are working on against the added information. You make an informed choice: pivot toward the new discovery and revisit prior stages or steps, include the information as a detail in the current project, or note the discovery for use in another project. Have no fear, this does not mean that you are starting over. There is no such thing as *failed research* if it results in *shared learning*. Celebrate the generation and sharing of information as discovery.

Note that the result of any process, project, or methodology is a point-in-time view of a situation. You should use the Compassion-Driven Innovation methodology regularly to continue to innovate and increase your understanding of our rapidly changing world.

Using Real-World Examples

Through the next four chapters, we'll teach you much more about how to execute the four stages introduced earlier. We'll illustrate the concepts with examples from three case studies:

- **Innovation: Africa.** Day-by-day since 2008, Founder and CEO Sivan Ya'ari has engaged African villagers, donors, and team members in her quest to deliver access to clean water, light, and solar energy to uplift the lives of more than three million people across 10 African countries. From the moment she saw first-hand the children who needed her help, through her studies in International Energy Management and Policy at Columbia University, to today, Sivan has been a source of inspiration to everyone she meets. The villagers she has helped have clean water, light, and power, along with health care, agriculture, commerce, and educational opportunities that were not possible in the absence of necessities. Sivan shows how you can make "good" even better through innovation fueled by compassion. Learn more about Sivan and her organization's journey at www.InnoAfrica.org.

- **Gutter Tex.** Co-owner Daniel Ouellette brings a passion for delivering first-class service to his clients and exceeding their expectations. Daniel's motto is "The only trace we leave is a job well done." Through 20 years of building businesses that offer premier solutions to homeowners, Daniel has found innovation at every inflection point of his interactions with employees, customers, and suppliers. A steady stream of five-star ratings, loyal employees whom customers praise by name, and quality results and guarantees speak to Daniel's intuitive ability to see what people need and give it to them. His ability to innovate in a service industry is grounded in the trust he has established both within his organization and from his customers. Daniel's success is proof that innovation is possible without inventing new products. Learn more about Daniel's operations in Central Texas at www.GutterTex.com.

- **AceraEI, an outreach program of Acera: The Massachusetts School for Science, Creativity and Leadership.** Courtney Dickinson believes that many common school practices induce student anxiety and reward students more for conformity and compliance rather than for innovation and problem-solving. Finding the public school system reluctant to change from within, she founded Acera School. There she creates a different learning experience based on individualized learning pathways, early and deep hands-on exposure to science, technology, engineering, art, and math (STEAM) topics, and the freedom to be creative and solve problems. This experience taps an intrinsic drive and empowers the leaders of tomorrow to reach their full potential. Through her outreach program, AceraEI, Courtney partners with public schools to improve the quality of education for all students through adoption of proven novel teaching methods, learning pedagogy, curricula, and tools. Learn more about AceraEI at www.EI.AceraSchool.org.

Summary

By honoring the philosophies of compassion, collaboration, wisdom, and prioritization, Compassion-Driven Innovation helps your team navigate through common innovation pitfalls. The methodology recognizes and provides guardrails for team building in the Include stage. It works to reduce the inherent anxiety responses[6] in collaborators via external validation in the Discover stage. It eliminates familiarity bias in design[7] in the Enlighten stage. It provides for collaborative engagement, right-resourcing, and implementation in the Activate stage. It also provides teams with a common language, inflection points, and checklists. By engaging teams in using Compassion-Driven Innovation, you will increase the likelihood of collaboration, innovation, and ultimate adoption of your team's work.

---

[6] A. Boyles. May 17, 2018. "What Anxiety Does to Us at Work." *Harvard Business Review*. https://hbr.org/2019/05/what-anxiety-does-to-us-at-work

[7] D. Burkus. July 07, 2015. "3 Ways Leaders Accidentally Undermine their Team's Creativity." *Harvard Business Review*. https://hbr.org/2015/07/3-ways-leaders-accidentally-undermine-their-teams-creativity

Stage 1: Include

Introduction to the Include Stage

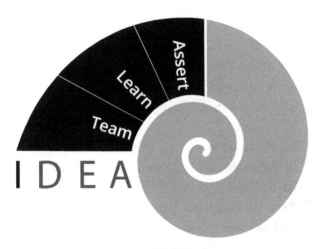

Figure 2.1 The Include stage

The Include (I) stage begins with forming a team that clarifies and unites around your theme or directive and learns from the genius that exists among members and readily available external sources (Figure 2.1). The team then crafts a story describing the affected personas and what their work or life is like as a result of challenges related to your theme. At the end of this stage, you will have created your initial proto-persona, proto-maps, and listed your assertions. You will be ready to interact with the external world as informed members of a community to gather unbiased feedback.

The next section illustrates a real-world example of using this checklist in the Include stage.

Include Checklist

Knowing what you are about to do can help you understand the how and why. For this reason, we provide a checklist at each stage that highlights the tasks to be completed. Don't worry; we'll explain what each of these checklist items mean and give you tips for getting started.

- ☐ Identify your project.
- ☐ Form your team.
    - ☐ Consider the initial problem the project is trying to solve.
    - ☐ Decide on the innovation type.
    - ☐ Determine discipline areas and skills of interest.
    - ☐ Build the team.
- ☐ Learn what exists.
    - ☐ Craft your theme(s) as a team.
    - ☐ Perform state-of-the-art research.
- ☐ Assert what you know.
    - ☐ Identify proto-personas.
    - ☐ Create proto-maps.
    - ☐ Write what you know.

Example of Innovation: Africa's Include Stage

Think about an organization such as Innovation: Africa when Sivan first set out to change the living conditions that she saw on a business trip to Africa. The theme she decided to follow is helping villages that are remote from the capital, remote from the grid, and are experiencing water scarcity. How might she have set about the Include stage? Jot down your own ideas and then compare them to these: The team leader forms a team that includes cross-discipline internal members and local experts who understand the challenges villagers face, along with possible high priority solutions, such as delivery of electricity or clean water. The team might consist of a project leader, solar and hydro engineers, and government and relief workers familiar with the living conditions and terrain of the area. The team documents the conditions which are more difficult, what has been done so far, and why that failed to meet expectations. They combine this information with data from secondary sources to quickly create situational awareness and a best guess about what problems to solve and how to solve them.

Identify Your Project

The Compassion-Driven Innovation methodology assumes that you are working on a project or have an idea of an area you are trying to improve. If you do not have an assigned project or mission, consider a project you are currently working on. What is the goal of the project? Are you trying to solve a specific problem? Hopefully that was a simple question to answer. If not, consider why the project exists. Describe what is expected from your team. Is there a specific type of challenge you want to solve? What is the timeframe for project completion?

Having a general idea of why you are innovating is required for deciding who to invite to the team.

Form Your Team

Forming a team is a luxury. Revel in it for a moment. You are in a situation in which you have the time, resources, and support to bring people together. While you are contemplating improvement, so many of our small business brethren are in a sinking ship using a paper cup to bail water, forced to make decisions in the moment, alone. Recognize how truly fortunate you are. Commemorate this opportunity by looking beyond the colleagues from your department or your last few projects.

Think deeply about who you can and should invite in because of their potential to contribute to this project. Look for new perspectives and expertise from people highly motivated to create meaningful change by exercising compassion for customers, team members, and themselves. The team members should be enthusiastic about having discussions on the topic you are exploring and demonstrate a collaborative and

compassionate spirit. Teams can thrive if they are comfortable sharing, learning, and pivoting together as their understanding of a challenge or problem increases.

Over the years, we have experienced other cyclical innovation methodologies and thinking paradigms. They can leave team members feeling expendable and isolated. While some methodologies consider empathy for the customer, we have seen times that the practice of those methodologies is done at the expense of the team members' mental and emotional well-being. Innovation without compassion for the team may produce great short-term results, but it leads to burnout and alienates the very people you need to make your organization successful.

Some organizations build innovation teams augmented with people from outside their company or organization. Others prefer recruiting only internal team members from diverse areas of expertise. Both approaches can be and have been successful.

Team forming and collaboration that is open to outside partnerships is widely researched by innovation luminary Henry Chesbrough. In cases in which an organization is receptive to external collaboration, we recommend taking the time to read Chesbrough's brilliant work on Open Innovation.[1] Should you choose open innovation, you will want to consider the various ways your organization is willing to bring innovation to market before you embark on team forming.

Internal team forming is equally well studied. These teams must include people with the accountability and skillset to drive your project forward. Research on forming effective innovation teams suggests that all team members have the basic skills of communication and interpersonal connection, because a single point of communication or bottleneck in communication is shown to decrease innovative team output. If you are interested in additional research, Google has published additional components of a good internal team.[2]

---

[1] H.W. Chesbrough. 2003. *Open Innovation: The New Imperative for Creating and Profiting from Technology* Harvard Business School Press. (Brown 2003).

[2] Google. "Re:Work." https://rework.withgoogle.com/print/guides/5721312655 835136/ (accessed April 24, 2021).

If you are reading this while in the midst of a project in which team members are already engaged, we do not recommend that you vote them off the island "Survivor-style" to make room for more informed, stronger, faster, or otherwise better equipped team members. No one is perfect, and rarely will anyone have every skill the team needs. We recommend that you use this section to determine what skills you have on the team and identify the additional skills you need to fill those gaps. As any project progresses, you will bring in new collaborators. This is expected and useful.

We recognize that expanding a team can feel risky because it can change the dynamics of the original team just as its members seem to have found a creative rhythm. They may feel that they were deemed inadequate to the task at hand, and that an "expert" will stride in and undermine their work or require them to rehash ideas they have already rejected.

We recommend that you set the expectation from the beginning of the project that additional resources will be tapped as needed, and that some resources may need to roll off the team once their expertise has been mined. You can reinforce these expectations by having transparent conversations to ensure that the team members understand what additional skills need to be added when the time comes, what skills can be released to other tasks, and what all team members will be expected to do at each step. Having this foundational understanding in place will increase team member's comfort level when it is time to bring in those new team members.

Understanding Your Team Needs

Working on complex challenges requires a variety of knowledge and skill sets. The size and number of people on your team will be related to the complexity and timeframe of your project. Research indicates that projects which require massive disruption should be led by small teams. Projects which are aimed at incremental problem-solving may be better done by larger teams.[3]

---

[3] D. Wang, and J.A. Evans. February 21, 2019. "Research: When Small Teams Are Better Than Big Ones." *Harvard Business Review.* https://hbr.org/2019/02/research-when-small-teams-are-better-than-big-ones

Consider the type of innovation you want to create. Do you want to disrupt the status quo, or do you want to creatively solve problems within an established paradigm? You can tell by considering the following:

- **Disruption** is a change in the way your organization, indus- try, or individuals fundamentally approach solving a need. Uber, AirBnB, and Amazon stand out as examples that disrupted the mobility, hospitality, and retail industries, respectively. These types of projects are often not projected to impact the bottom line in the short term, but the payoffs can be huge in the longer term. If the payoff is expected in a strategic rather than tactical timeframe and is vague or open-ended, lean toward forming a team capable of delivering disruptive innovation.
- **Incremental problem-solving** is tackling specific challenges or a series of challenges within an industry or organization. Is your challenge reasonably well defined or understood? Do you anticipate that this team's findings will result in shorter-term direct changes to the business, products, or other area? If so, lean toward problem-solving.

If you are aiming for disruption, you should start with a core team of three to four people. This allows for fast collaboration, iteration, and pivoting. Look for team members interested and knowledgeable about the areas you are investigating. You will only use the following Core Team Questions.

If you are tasked with incremental problem-solving, you will need to expand your team beyond the core three to four people. Research shows that larger teams are more effective at delivering incremental innovation in more established markets. Use the Core Questions that follow and add the Extended Team questions listed as follows to help identify who you should include.

Before looking at the questions below, be honest with yourself. How much knowledge do you have about the subject? What skills do you bring to the team? What additional knowledge and skills are needed for establishing a well-rounded view of the situation from beginning to end? An objective assessment will yield a vastly better result.

Core Team Questions:

- What areas are your project trying to understand? Narrow it down by creating a list of industries, use cases, technology, or other aspects.
- Which part of the list above is most critical to the project at hand? Prioritize two to three aspects.
- Who currently has a deep and broad understanding of best-in-class offerings or practices in the prioritized aspects?
- If you have a specific set of technologies to consider, can you identify experts in the fields of study (such as technology, tooling, or manufacturing)?
- Do you have someone who excels at finding and interviewing customers and industry experts?
- Do you have access to someone skilled in storytelling and written communication of nonconcrete ideas?
- Can you find a team member who has a skill of visual thinking and attention to detail to document critical linkages through visualization techniques?
- Who is passionate about solving the topic at hand?

Extended Team Questions:

Add these on to the Core Team questions above when your project is aimed toward problem-solving rather than disruption.

- Who are your internal stakeholders for adopting innovation in this area?
- If you anticipate the result is something that will be brought to a customer, internal or external, who understands the complexities of go-to-market or internal adoption?
- Who internally would be significantly impacted by solving the problem at hand?

- Would solving this result in a need for changes in customer messaging?
- Would solving this result in a need to alter sales or go-to-market models?
- Which internal customers are advocating for understanding of the topic at hand?
- Is someone on your team great at creating organizational buy-in and knowing who to keep in the loop?

Example of Team Members for Innovation: Africa

In 2008, Sivan composed a small core team to create a disruptive innovation that would transform the lives of rural villagers in Africa. Her short-term goal would be focused on a single village at a time, with a longer goal of making meaningful change across rural Africa.

For their disruptive innovation in October 2008, the core team included Sivan and three other individuals:

- **Founder and CEO:** sets the theme, mission, objectives; leads the strategy and planning; conducted the initial fundraising, negotiations, and management for the first Innovation: Africa projects; oversees ongoing operations.
- **Associate Executive Director:** oversees projects and programs in the organization.
- **Lawyer:** a pro-bono attorney who filed for tax-exempt status and researched African laws regarding importing solar panels tax-free.
- **Solar Power Consultant:** Sivan's professor from Columbia University.

Over the years, Sivan's team has pivoted to focus on solving a series of incremental challenges. One of these is determining how and when to expand into new countries. To answer this question, they added external stakeholders to their team, including:

- **The ambassador to the UN:** to help choose the right region.

- **Ministers of Water, Energy, and Health:** who are familiar with the living conditions and terrain of the area and can help with setting priorities either to help first with access to clean water or electricity to medical centers and schools.

In addition, Innovation: Africa employees, including a Director and a Deputy Country Director, are responsible for hiring local African employees whose roles include:

- **Country Director:** manages the local Country Managers and Project Managers in the country of assignment as well as the relations with local contractors. The Country Directors are also responsible for overseeing daily fieldwork, project installations, maintenance issues, monthly budgets, expense reports, and bookkeeping. Moreover, they are committed to regular travel and field visits. While in the field, Country Directors prepare for donor trips, record field notes, oversee project implementation, meet with local contractors, visit prospective projects, meet with relevant stakeholders and ministers, and accompany international guests on project visits.
- **Deputy Country Director:** assists the Country Director in managing the local team in the research, implementation, and monitoring of solar and water projects across rural Africa. Commits to regular travel to Africa. While in the field, assists in preparations for donor trips, records field notes, oversees project implementation, meets with local contractors, visits prospective projects, meets with relevant stakeholders and ministers, and accompanies international guests on project visits.

Local employees in Africa include:

- **Local Country Manager:** responsible for managing operations across two regional offices and overseeing the coordination, monthly budgets, accounting, project delivery, strategy, and report to the Country Director in Israel.

- **Regional Managers:** oversee and manage the daily activities of each regional team, working directly with the municipality and serving as the point of contact with all contractors as a regional supervisor.
- **Field Officers:** work directly with the community to sensitize and mobilize villagers for project installation and maintenance. In addition, field officers conduct post installation monitoring and evaluation and work closely with the communities during regular visits to ensure the smooth operation of the system and the microbusinesses launched by the villagers.
- **Electrical Engineers:** oversee all installation and maintenance of solar projects.
- **Civil Engineers:** supervise the water tower construction in accordance with the approved blueprints to ensure Innovation: Africa standards are upheld.
- **Water Engineers:** implement the water system design, including the type and size of the pumps, the piping systems, and the number of taps to ensure enough supply of water to accommodate the needs of the community.
- **Hydrogeologists:** to supervise the geophysical survey and drilling at each village.

Example of Team Members for Gutter Tex

Co-owner Daniel Ouellette built Gutter Tex on a commitment to customer satisfaction and high-quality craftsmanship. When hiring, he considers the long-term relationship that he wants to generate with each employee. He has built processes that help ensure each hire is the kind of person who values teamwork, quality craftsmanship, and the ability to have positive interactions that build homeowner trust. In return, he provides training, opportunities for growth, and an environment built on mutual respect.

When he was ready to expand his operations, he chose to find innovation in his existing geographic markets rather than expanding to other areas. He knew that meant making improvements in marketing, sales, and customer interactions. To help him with this incremental innovation objective, he formed a team that included these members:

- **Chief Operating Officer:** expert in the specific services offered, the sales model, and establishing the installation process.
- **Technology Expert:** responsible for architecting the sales and ordering software platform.
- **User Experience Expert:** skilled at innovation, visualization, and communication of ideas.
- **Marketing Expert:** runs the website, does search engine optimization, and manages advertising to drive sales.

Example of Team Members for AceraEI

In Courtney's initial steps to transform the learning experience for children in public schools, she was met with leadership changes and program cancellations beyond her control. She realized that she needed to create an environment that could serve as a catalyst for change. She founded Acera School to invent and pilot test innovative education approaches and founded AceraEI to partner with public schools across the nation wanting to implement the resulting tools and techniques. To enable the disruptive innovation needed, the AceraEI core team consisted of these members:

- **Founder:** established the mission and method; identified the challenges and concepts for reimagining the way schools can address education; frames priorities, plans budget, champions school district relationships and customization philosophy, articulates and evolving the messaging and focus to support public school uptake and fundraising; evangelizes the need, mission, and success stories.
- **Development Team:** plans and conducts fundraising activities; part time expertise from multiple people in identifying and building relationships to solicit donations from individuals and organizations/organizational foundations. This skill set is spread across multiple volunteers: a key board member with connections in the life sciences space, the school founder, and

the development lead from the school who is an expert in educational fundraising.

- **Director:** responsible for project management and thought leader partnerships for 25 percent of his time. The other 75 percent is focused on fundraising for the Acera School core program.
- **Strategic Initiatives Manager:** assesses and adapts approaches for measuring success in education, educational initiatives, and partnership programs; provides a systems view and program assessment which broadens the definition of "school success" in quantifiable and scalable ways.

To round out the skill sets, they consulted as needed with teacher specialists to build, pilot, and document novel science, technology, engineering, arts, and mathematics education (STEAM) curricula and facilitate public school teacher training workshops.

Knowing how to find people who have a specific skill early on is helpful: otherwise forming the team takes time and you may end up leading multiple roles on your own at the same time.

As you can see from these examples, the composition of a team should support the goals and the subject areas in which you are innovating.

Build Compassion in Your Team Through Connection

Research shows that familiarity increases emotional engagement in the aforementioned examples, music.[4] Research also shows that people are more likely to be attracted to that which is familiar.[5] We suggest that familiarity could also increase our ability to engage and appreciate the

---

[4] C.S. Pereira, J. Teixeira, P. Figueiredo, J. Xavier, S.L. Castro, and E. Brattico. 2011. "Music and Emotions in the Brain: Familiarity Matters." *PLoS ONE* 6, no. 11, e27241. https://journals.plos.org/plosone/article?id=10.1371/journal.pone.0027241

[5] C., Lumen. 2021. "ER Services: Introduction to Pathology. Module 10: Social Psychology. Attraction and Love." https://courses.lumenlearning.com/suny-fmcc-intropsych/chapter/prosocial-behavior/#:~:text=One%20of%20the%20reasons%20why,will%20be%20attracted%20to%20them (accessed April 24, 2021).

skills and disciplines of others. We have found that the more we understand the people who are performing jobs different from ours, the more deeply we see the value of the work they do.

Consider how much you know about the various roles in your organization. Get to know people in diverse types of jobs, on different teams, and with different points of view. Seek to understand the value and experience necessary to excel in those roles. That job that someone makes look easy is likely a discipline which was built over years of deep passion and learning. Over time, this practice may also help you understand who could be impactful in future innovation projects.

Should you choose to engage in a more open innovation approach, think about how you can meet people across your industry. Summits, networking events, meetups, open source groups, and forums are among the many ways to engage and expand your community. Examine ways you could help colleagues achieve their aspirations. You may be surprised at what people are interested in and working on.

Consider Team Dynamics

As important as the skills we outline above, consider peoples' preferences. Not everyone is well-suited to or likes collaboration. Do not ask a fish to ride a bike and do not judge it for choosing to swim. The goal here is to let people shine with the talents they have in the way that makes sense for them, not to force everyone into one mold.

Unless individuals who prefer to be lone wolves are interested in expanding their people skills, consider including them as consultants to the project on an as-needed basis, rather than including them as core team members. On the other hand, some people prefer consensus over challenging the assumption of others. This will be a liability in the first three stages of Compassion-Driven Innovation, when it is necessary to challenge assumptions. However, they are usually well suited to augment and strengthen the team in the final stage of the methodology, Activate, when consensus-building is key. Engage consensus builders early and individually, then keep them up to date on the project so they are thinking about how to help when you reach the Activate stage.

Internal competition can be healthy, but we would like to warn you that it sometimes ends in disaster. Politics and turf wars are well-known challenges in organizational innovation.[6] In one consulting engagement, Reineke encountered an innovation team who started to behave as if the rest of an organization was a competitor. People outside of the innovation team started to behave as if the innovation team was a threat. This was easily recognized via the disparaging remarks against the behaviors and performance of both the innovation and product teams. Instead of building bridges and bringing in people with the political and social acumen to create unity, the internal innovators isolated themselves from the larger organization. The result was disastrous. The innovation team had discovered, prototyped, and patented an innovative solution that customers wanted. However, the team failed to engage the rest of the organization, and the project was shuttered. If you work in an organization where this may happen, extend your core team to include someone who is great at creating organizational allies. This person can enable you to achieve organizational buy-in when you reach the Activate stage. Without them, no matter how exceptional your project may be, you run the risk of having it terminated for political reasons.

Another unforeseen force that can sabotage your project is how credit is given or taken. As you innovate through iterative understanding, the final creative leap in a design or solution often builds on the small leaps of innovation that have occurred throughout the project. In a culture where credit is readily shared among team members, this is a win–win in which all contributors throughout the project gain value from the outcome and individuals understand that credit goes to the group. In a culture in which credit is seen as being sliced from a pie that is limited in quantity and not for sharing, you will need to reach agreements up front from the team about how credit will be handled. One individual claiming credit for the team's work can undo weeks or months of team building and collaborative success. Compassion-Driven Innovation can thrive only where cannibalism and credit-stealing are squelched from the outset.

---

[6] S. Kirsner. 2019. "What Companies that are Good at Innovation Get Right." *Harvard Business Review.* https://hbr.org/2019/11/what-companies-that-are-good-at-innovation-get-right

Activity: Put Team into Action

☐ Determine whether your current project is closer to disruption or problem-solving.

☐ Determine which skills you currently have on the team, including yours. Determine who can best augment your team to fill in the skills that you need.

☐ Propose the list as the initial core team. Revisit the core team members if there is a missing skill set. Teams may be expanded or changed as a project becomes clearer.

☐ Determine how your organization will deal with credit and incentives for your team to align with your organizations' goals and culture.

Learn What Exists

Assuming you are not building a Jurassic-era dinosaur park (which ultimately ends in the professional demise of you and your colleagues), one way to accelerate innovation is to stand on the shoulders of geniuses who have paved a path before you. You can use the knowledge and discipline of your organization and of the industries in which you are innovating in two ways:

- **Theme**—By building on your teams' foundational assertions for your project, which are intrinsically motivating and based on compassion, your organization, and the directives or organizational goals that are imperatives within your charter.
- **State-of-the-art**—By understanding best-in-class solutions that currently exist and researching thought leadership about the future state of the areas related to your theme.

Do not mistake learning from and building on the work of others with stealing. We are not asserting that we should adhere to any findings as restrictions or claim them as our own. The Learn step uses the knowledge of the past to establish baseline credibility. We then build on what is of value, and always with proper attribution.

Craft Your Theme

Together, your newly formed team must create your written statement of your theme. This statement is an actionable *point-in-time understanding of your project and organizational directive.*

You will note that there are two parts to that description. The first is obvious—a description of what you think the project is supposed to accomplish. The second is less obvious, but we have learned over the years that it is just as important. If your strategic initiative is not aligned to your organization's directive, even if you have the most amazing innovations of all time, it may fail to gain internal traction. You cannot heel-click your way out of that kind of a mess. In most cases, "no internal traction" means "no launched innovation."

A good theme sparks a team's intrinsic motivation and is based on compassion about who you want to help. It must be specific enough to bring a project focus but does not impose a solution. In case you are not familiar with creating great themes for projects, we provide example nonleading questions below to help you get started. Exceptional texts and research are available online if the prompts we provide do not result in a theme that meets your needs.

You will refer back to your theme when prioritizing your findings throughout the project. It can be useful to consider the theme as your project guardrails.

To write your theme statement, you will:

- Identify at least one overarching statement that describes the goals of the project.
- Identify and align that statement to one or more of your organization's strategic directives.
- Consider your team's goals.

- List the overarching areas and challenges you are trying to solve.
- Describe the challenges without listing the solutions.
- Describe the principles you agree to follow when researching or solving the challenges.
- Consider your organizations' goals.
- List your organization's strategic goals—long- and short-term.
- Consider the goals of your group in general.

Combine the team and organization goals and draft your theme statement. No one-size-fits-all formula can deliver an impactful and meaningful theme for your organization. Some themes drive new products or highlight organizational principles. Some extend a larger initiative. Some aspire to change culture. A company may define themes without a clear understanding of what they are going to deliver to meet the goal. This fluidity is healthy and natural. Consider the examples below as you craft your project theme.

Example of Innovation: Africa Theme

Sivan conducted research and found that more than 600 million people in Africa did not have access to electricity. She was also particularly moved by a photo of the African continent and Europe at night. While Europe is ablaze with light in the photograph, Africa is predominantly dark. This drove the theme for Innovation: Africa:

Provide access to safe and clean water and electricity to rural villages that are remote from the capital, are not connected to the grid and do not have a reliable source of safe drinking water.

This theme became the guardrails for the organization, every time she had to select the next village either in an existing country or a new country. She used this theme to guide her team in making the final decision.

Example of Gutter Tex Theme

Gutter Tex is a locally owned business in Texas. They have a unique technology that creates on-demand, high-quality seamless gutters for

homeowners using rivets instead of screws. This results in a solution with a longer lifetime and superior performance that can stand up to the torrential rains that randomly strike in the Austin and San Antonio, Texas, areas.

Gutter Tex has a large customer base with hundreds of five-star reviews. However, they want to grow their business and make their process more efficient for their customers and employees.

If we were thinking about this from just a sales perspective, we could create a Gutter Tex project theme such as:

Increase the number and types of customers in the homeowner segment who could have access to the high-quality service we provide.

That is a good start, but it does not capture the essence of what Daniel is trying to achieve through innovation. To add more color and help generate a higher level of intrinsic motivation, we could align the statement with larger organizational directives, business focus, or strategic goals. In this case, their organizational directives include:

- Delight customers above all else.
- Ensure happy crews and team members.
- Increase business by 25 percent in the next 24 months.

Using these directives, they can update their theme to:

Find new ways to delight customers through improved customer experience when accessing high-quality Gutter Tex services, while innovating on our employees' experience.

This theme gives us a clearer picture of the project with guardrail goals.

Example of AceraEI Theme

AceraEI has the mission to transform public schools by introducing early and deep exposure to STEAM topics, along with systems thinking, problem-solving, and creativity to help students become the best version of themselves. Following is a list of some of the ways the AceraEI team frames the differences in philosophy between the public school system and AceraEI:

Traditional Model = Age-Based Standards	AceraEI Model = Individualized Discovery
Learning = Coverage of state specified content, defined by age-based standards.	Learning = Inquiry-based, built around student passions and capacity.
Focused on foundational knowledge.	Focused on complex thinking.
Teach to the middle; cover content.	Individualize; cultivate curiosity.
Teacher as lecturer and primary source of information.	Teacher as facilitator with access to world-class scientists and mentors.
Convergent thinking; memorization of facts; predefined methods and approaches.	Divergent, creative problem-solving with links to real-world challenges; meaningful work.
Subject areas that are divided and distinct.	Multidisciplinary learning that engages students in ways that add meaning and purpose.
The reward for learning is extrinsic, measured by performance on standardized tests.	The reward for learning is intrinsic, measured by the engagement and motivation of the student to learn, explore and connect ideas.

The theme of AceraEI is to: *Provide students with meaningful learning at school by teaching them habits like systems thinking, problem solving, creativity, persistence, emotional intelligence, and initiative, which will set them up for success in life.* AceraEI created a practical way to follow this theme by crystalizing innovative teaching methods into "Tools to Transform Schools," along with a dashboard to measure school success. Following this methodology, public school leaders catalyze change by attending workshops to identify tools and priorities, identify outcome-based success criteria, and participate in a repeating school engagement process to adopt the tools to best fit into their unique school settings.

Perform State-of-the-Art Research

We have all seen those films where a group of underdogs coat themselves in matchy–matchy warpaint and, over the course of two hours, with little skill or planning, they attack and beat an enemy army who out-skills and out-numbers them. While this may seem like a glorious way to win a

Activity: Put Theme into Action

- ☐ Brainstorm with your team and write down variants of your theme.
- ☐ Vote and combine content until your team feels that the statement represents what you have come together to do. Ensure you include your organizational goals.
- ☐ At the end of this activity, make sure the team knows the theme and is familiar with any other organizational themes that are relevant and appropriate.

As you move forward, refer back to ensure that the activities and challenges you pursue continue to align to the project theme.

battle (um, no), the reality is that in the absence of scripting and editing, teams need to study, plan, and upskill to increase the likelihood of a win. In Compassion-Driven Innovation, once you understand the theme in which you want to innovate, you list the general areas of technology or industry information that you need to understand. This will define the state-of-the-art research.

The Compassion-Driven Innovation methodology views the synthesis of knowledge about what exists today as a vital step toward understanding what *should* exist. State-of-the-art research is not an *output;* it is an *input.* When you use this research and industry awareness as an input to inform your project, you can have enlightened conversations with the right people. You will become well-versed in topics related to your theme and be able to ask meaningful questions that yield deeper insights.

Imagine for a moment what would happen if you skipped state-of-the-art research before conducting interviews with potential customers or other experts. You would undoubtedly spend time asking questions about information that was easily attainable if you had read a few reports. You would have wasted the time and good will of experts who agreed to be interviewed, and who are unlikely to make their calendars available to you next time you need their help. These missteps would likely lead to a lack of credibility, and your innovative ideas may lose internal traction.

As critical as the state-of-the-art understanding step is, it alone is insufficient for you to formulate your innovation. Doing so creates the trap of designing solutions based on what you see in the market. This approach is shortsighted, incremental, and rarely yields innovation. Using unexamined knowledge dooms us to repeat past mistakes.

Your goal during this step of the Include stage is to gather enough data to have informed conversations about the theme you are working with. Next, you will summarize your understanding in artifacts, which are described in more detail below. You will then use these artifacts to onboard new team members as your project requires, or to establish a collective understanding of the fields of study related to your theme. Good state-of-the-art research will help your team pull from the reserve of likely applicable forward-looking ideas as examples of what you could or should not do to solve the challenges.

The format you use to share findings must match how your organization is most comfortable learning. Among the most common artifacts are briefing documents, slides, memoranda, or videos. We will generically refer to this content as *artifacts*. Regardless of which format you choose to create your outputs, you must place them into a common repository that is appropriately governed and controlled while also being accessible by those who need access throughout the project.

Create State-of-the-Art Artifacts

When you are in a small organization in which the researchers will also serve as the implementers, the emphasis on artifacts may not seem worthwhile. But even in this situation, you will at times need to come back to what you have learned to educate those who hold the budget decisions, and bring others up to date on the project to ensure ongoing buy-in. And if you are in an existing organization where you do not know everyone by name, then you need to sit forward and pay close attention to this: Particularly in large organizations, you need to create enough of a "paper trail" to show what you have learned, how it influenced your thinking, why it drove you to the conclusions you made. You will specifically revisit these artifacts when you present your innovation in the Activate stage.

One of the benefits of including a marketing expert on your team or as collaborators early on is that they tend to be experts on how to communicate information. Talk to someone with the communication strength and brainstorm a few ways that you can make sure everyone is able to find and understand your state-of-the-art research.

New to Research?

We see a lot of research responsibilities being handed off to third-party analysts or consultants for many reasons. Perhaps you do not have the skills to set up or conduct research on your own, or it simply seems more efficient to outsource it given your time constraints. It is true that many organizations aren't equipped to conduct unbiased, ethical research. And, research that explores new territory or pushes the boundaries of current understanding requires adherence to standards of conduct and ethics. Researchers dedicate years (and often lifetimes) to achieve mastery. Even then, they utilize standards, boards, peer review, auditing, attestation, and duplication of work before claiming knowledge. You can and should learn more about these topics over time, but probably not today. For today, and for your project at hand, unless you are a trained researcher, consider your objective to be data gathering.

We are going to revisit the list you created in the "Forming a Team" section. (Forgot? Answer the questions: What areas is your project trying to understand? Can you create a list of industries, use cases, technology, or other aspects? Which areas related to your theme did you prioritize?)

For each of those areas, we suggest starting with four main categories of research:

- Internal conversations.
- External industry and competitive landscape.
- Academic, government, or nonprofit publications.
- Open-source software, programs, or collaborative community research.

Conversations

If we had a dollar for every person who claimed that no one in their organization has a clue, we estimate we would have $42 (After all, "42" is the answer to the big question.)[7] The Compassion-Driven Innovation leadership mindset asks that you set aside the notion that you are surrounded by clueless individuals.

Many people have interest, knowledge, and connections on the subject you are researching. We are betting that some are in your extended organization. Set up brief meetings with people who may have some interest or insight into the areas you are researching. Describe the areas you are looking into. Ask them to share what they know about your areas of research. Do they have resources they use to learn about the latest trends or products?

Consider looking for existing information in your marketing, sales, or engineering organizations. What does your team already know about the theme or customers who may be impacted by the theme? Is there documentation about journeys or personas that you can use as a starting point?

Remember, you are not looking for *answers*. You are looking for leads to useful insights, resources, and connections. You do not need to know more than the people you are engaging. Ask them about their perceptions. Ask if they have pointers to information, people, or organizations to explore. Start simply. All we are asking you to do is to start a conversation and let people know what you are looking into. You never know where it may lead.

If you are lucky enough to work in an organization with a research or strategy team, read existing papers they have produced and set up conversations with those subject matter experts. Researchers often have archives and relevant predigested information on which your team can build.

Internal conversations serve two purposes: to increase your area of knowledge and enable moments of serendipity which can only occur through interpersonal connection. Innovation thrives in long-term relationships. If someone provides you with data, find a way to credit them in the research. Always include attribution. Always ensure that you express gratitude. One sure way to destroy your team's chance of having your innovation adopted by your organization is to be perceived as taking without giving back.

---

[7] Wikipedia: The Free Encyclopedia. 2021. "Phrases from the Hitchhiker's Guide to the Galaxy." https://en.wikipedia.org/wiki/Phrases_from_The_Hitchhiker%27s_Guide_to_the_Galaxy (accessed April 24, 2021).

This is also a great time to start making a wish list of team members you may want to collaborate with in the future. Did any of the conversations result in a 1+1=3 feeling? We always keep a list of collaborators for future inclusion.

External Industry and Competitive Landscape

The research you conduct on industry players related to your theme can be of significant value. You will want to understand how companies position themselves and their capabilities, as well as which startups have received funding in areas you are investigating and what their approach is. Knowing who your customers and prospects are talking to and what their impressions are will guide you forward.

If you are unsure which organizations to research, talk to your sales teams and your partners. Chances are they run into your competitors. Industry analysts can be another easy place to start if you are unsure of the players in a market. Analysts often provide weighted (sometimes pay-to-play) lists of companies in a market and the value that they bring to customers. You can download reports that list offerings and competitive differentiators of each player.

One of the beauties of the remote and touchless sales process shifts in recent years is that you can often find demonstration videos, complete user manuals, support forums, and tools online. Remember to discern the reality of what is available from the vision a company is selling. Interpret company-posted and sponsored whitepapers as well-crafted messaging. Don't dismiss them, however, because well-crafted messaging can be a differentiator you shouldn't ignore.

Academia

University researchers are creative and generous partners. If your organization is lucky enough to have ties into academia, consider attending research informational sessions and requesting conversations around research that applies to your areas of interest. Find out whether you have an academic liaison, they are often able to set conversations up for you. Keep an open mind; like all inventions, those in academia may be presented under the guise of one perspective and can be leveraged in a completely novel manner to advance other areas. If you can partner, attribution and collaboration are essential.

If you do not have direct access to university or college programs, dozens of academic research paper portals offer access to the latest in innovation. For example, *Semantic Scholar* is an online search tool you can use to discover research.[8]

You also can find repositories where many scientists and researchers publish work and research directly; another option is access to research archives with the stipulation that the work is awaiting peer review.

Government, Standards, Open Source, and Communities

In an acknowledged general waving of our hands, following is a collection of other places you should consider investigating:

- Government-funded research projects and standards are particularly prevalent in the EU. This research is usually conducted in conjunction with academia, industry, and global cooperatives. When casting your net for research reports, consider the source, the objectives, and who provided the research funding. This will help you make informed interpretations of the data.
- Standards boards and law may be interesting areas to research. Some themes will overlap with upcoming or existing standards. Consider which may impact your company and buyers (even if outside of the immediate theme or areas of research).
- Open source communities are prevalent in forward-looking technology areas and in areas of social interest. Myriad reasons exist to join and participate in open source, and there are some reasons to keep your company name and work out of it.
- Consider looking toward communities as well. Industry or interest-specific sites and forums often host member articles. These publications can prove important for understanding technologies, research trends and getting ahead of the curve, but should also be taken for what it is—thought leadership.

---

[8] Semantic Scholar. www.semanticscholar.org/ (accessed April 24, 2021).

Use Advanced Research When Possible

Some organizations are large enough to have entire teams dedicated to the practice of understanding and advancing state-of-the-art often resulting in inventions. You can use the Compassion-Driven Innovation methodology to bridge the gap between inventions and what your customer base may adopt (innovation). Find out what state-of-the-art information exists which intersects with your theme and consider who you may want to work with in the future. If you can leverage this research, you can often push your company forward together.

Consider the challenges encountered by the organization Innovation: Africa. The invention of solar panel batteries had the potential to be life-changing for remote areas. However, in their first project, Sivan discovered that the way she proposed to use the invention was not *relatable*. She proposed supplying lights to medical centers and then learned that the lack of fresh water was an overarching issue that needed to be resolved first. When she uncovered this knowledge, she pivoted to dig wells with solar-powered pumps that provided water to villages from underground aquifers. This innovation was meaningful to the villagers, who readily collaborated and learned how to service the pumps and solar panels.

Assert What You Know

You have collected a massive amount of data. Using the knowledge gained from Learn, you will roughly sketch, quite literally, what you know and what you do not know. This is a critical step that forms the basis of the Discover stage.

This is most easily done by:

- **Identifying proto-personas**[9]—Make a best guess at who is impacted by your theme based on what you know.

---

[9] We would like to note that the techniques that the Compassion-Driven Innovation methodology recommends using in this step are not new. The concept of personas is widely attributed to Alan Cooper's publication in the early 1980s. The first occurrence of journey maps is frequently attributed to Jan Carlzon or to Lewis Carbone and Stephan Haeckel's 1994 article# referencing "experience blue-

Activity: Put State-of-the-Art into Action

☐ Use the list of markets, offerings, and technologies you prioritized in the "Team" and "Theme" sections as a starting point.

☐ Document the current state of these areas as they relate to your theme and organization's objectives.

☐ Highlight any specific language your customers and industry experts are using.

☐ Determine where you will store your research.

☐ Determine what formats the research should be in.

Assign each team member an area to investigate. For each area do:

☐ Internal conversations
☐ External discovery
☐ Academic review
☐ Community research.

Consider creating rankings, tables, or other easy-rating mechanisms to make the information easier to consume or understand.

As a team, review and discuss the state-of-the-art research content to ensure that everyone has a similar level of understanding about what exists today and likely future developments.

- **Drawing proto-maps**—Create a best guess sketch of known relationships and persona behaviors within your theme and learning.

---

print." We openly commemorate the innovations of all of the brilliant researchers and thinkers who popularized and paved the way for these tools. We lay no claim to their creation. If you would like to read about user experience, persona and mapping techniques, hundreds of books and courses specialize in them.

- **Writing your knowns and unknowns**—List your assertions, ideas, and gaps in understanding.

Identify Proto-Personas

The Compassion-Driven Innovation methodology greatly simplifies two well-known user experience (UX)[10] concepts:

- **Personas**—a fictional representation of a type of person(s) or entity is related to the project.
- **Proto-personas**—a dramatically simplified shell that simply provides a name for a group of people you intend to better understand.

Personas are typically high-fidelity, detailed representations of a group or target customers. Their goal is to help you understand the needs of the different stakeholders that will be using the solution you are innovating, as buyers, users, observers, and so on. They are both an art form and a science. You are not building robust personas yet. In this step, you create nothing more than named shells that represent groups of people who are impacted by your project. Some user experience experts refer to this as a prototyped persona (proto-persona). More important than knowing all the personas is simply identifying who may be the most important buyer or user persona impacted by your theme as a proto-persona. This is a useful means to an end.

Think of your current project and write a list of the general types of people or roles who are:

- Directly impacted;
- Indirectly impacted;
- Influencers of those who are impacted.

---

[10] For discussion on this topic, see www.nngroup.com/articles/definition-user-experience/

Example of Proto-Personas for Innovation: Africa

- **Impacted village community**
- **Donors** who pay for the privilege to support a village
- **Influencers who provide the support**
  o Innovation: Africa employees
  o Contractors
- **Influencers who help to choose the village** that will get the support
  o Ambassadors in the United Nations (UN)
  o District officers
  o The chief and the village community
  o Innovation: Africa-assigned team

Example of Proto-Personas for Gutter Tex

- **"Personal relationship-driven" homeowner**—likely to want an in-person consultation and desires to know the team that would be providing the service.
- **"No hassles" homeowner**—likely to want a fully automated experience that does not involve meeting sales team members or installation engineers.
- **Building owner**—person who owns real estate that is not used as a primary residence; wants efficiency and quality.
- **Employee: Sales Representative**—desires to give accurate quotes in an efficient manner.
- **Employee: Installation Engineer**—desires to provide high-quality installation for the most homeowners with the least driving between jobs.

Example of Proto-Personas for AceraEI

- **The students in the selected school to be transformed**
- **Influencers who provide the support**
  o AceraEI—Acera Education Innovation change agent teacher team

- o The selected school leadership
- o The selected school transformation teacher team.
- Influencers who help to choose the school that will get the support.

Leadership of schools who are philosophically aligned with AceraEI learning approaches in situations where funds can be raised to pay for the change management process and teacher training workshops.

- Influencers who help to decide which tools should be used to transform the school
  - o AceraEI—Acera Education Innovation change agent teacher team
  - o The selected school leadership
  - o The selected school transformation teacher team.
- Buyers—Parents—pay taxes so expect to their child to get a good education
- Donors—Educational philanthropists who believe in AceraEI's approach who want to see it shared in the public education space.

Create Proto-Maps

In the Include stage, the Compassion-Driven Innovation methodology tiptoes into visualizing your theme and what you know about what exists in a theme by creating two maps. In this case, a map is just a sketch or visual representation of ideas. We have found that of all the user experience maps that *can* be used in this step, two are the most useful: a relationship map and a proto-journey map.

- A *relationship map* is exactly what it sounds like—it shows how personas relate to each other. Within a relationship map, you may have an influencer map, a buyer map, and an impact map.
  - o An *influencer map* is a direct representation of those who may affect buyers.

- o A *buyer map* is a direct representation of those who consume a good or service.
- o An *impact map* identifies the effects on the buyer map.
- *A proto-journey map* is a simplified view of the lifecycle that you understand about the theme. It illustrates the provider's perspective of the journey. It is your best informed guess on how the customer journey map should be.

Before building the maps, restate your understanding of the customer's current challenges or needs and the theme which you are pursuing.

To illustrate a relationship map, you may have something as simple as a series of names and arrows that connect personas to each other and categorize their relationship, such as this relationship map shown for Innovation: Africa (Figure 2.2).

Relationship maps increase your ability to understand the people or entities involved in the challenge you are trying to solve. Consider your project and create a few variations of simple relationship maps. Then try to identify any missing personas.

The goal is to simply get a high-level sketch of the personas to keep in mind as you move forward to write your assertions.

To create a proto-journey map, sketch one version of the life cycle of how your organization could solve the customer needs related to your theme. Label the order in which you perceive activities occurring. Simple prompts for this include: Who would take an action? What would they do? What order would they do it in? This map represents how the proto-personas will interact from day zero until the end of your solution's useful life. See Figure 2.3.

At the end of this exercise, you should have a very basic view of the *people* impacted by your theme and a very basic view of the *journey* your company and customer may take related to your theme. You will now use this to create a list of what you *know*.

Example of Proto-Maps for Gutter Tex

From the outset, Daniel realized that the business had to be built on positive references from other area homeowners. He had seen too many

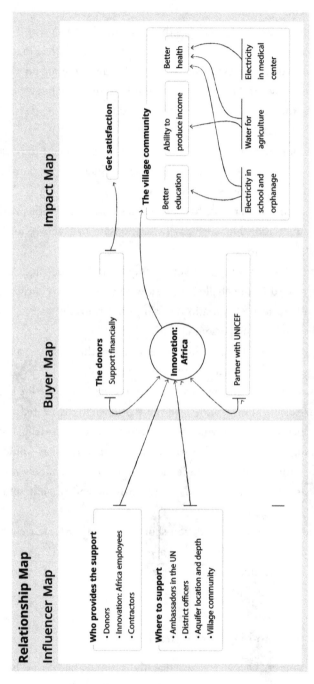

Figure 2.2 Innovation: Africa relationship map

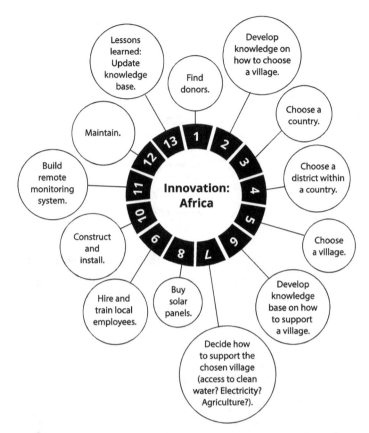

Figure 2.3 Innovation: Africa proto-journey map from the provider perspective

service businesses trying to scale without consideration for quality or positive customer experiences. Daniel took time to understand the influencers and realized that he needed a way to ensure that every customer could be a reference. The proto-journey that follows illustrates the solution delivery experience that accounts for their existing business. Following is a simple sketch of what they may have considered to be the relationship map at the beginning of the process of innovating on their business (Figure 2.4).

To take his business further, he also gained a clear understanding of what the typical process was for a home service. He identified all the touchpoints between the customer and his business and trained every

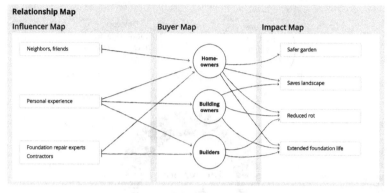

Figure 2.4 Gutter Tex proto-relationship map

employee how to interact in a way that is ethical and positive for both the company and the customer. And we could imagine an initial proto-journey map as shown in Figure 2.5.

Figure 2.5 Gutter Tex proto-journey map

Example of Proto-Maps for AceraEI

From her prior efforts to transform the public school system organically, Courtney understood that the obvious "buyers" included school authorities. But she also realized that the parents within the school system are direct buyers. And when AceraEI needed funding to scale the transformation, a third set of "buyers" emerged—the donors who supported her nonprofit cause. To date, all AceraEI programs have been funded privately, so in choosing partner schools, the AceraEI team must place an emphasis on schools with fundraising abilities to pay for programming.

Courtney also took time to think through the many groups of influencers. A simple sketch of what her relationship map at the beginning of the process might have looked like the following (Figure 2.6).

Proto-journey maps can be as specific or as general as is appropriate for the situation. Following is an illustration of Courtney's journey, which includes the full life cycle of her education initiative (Figure 2.7).

Write What You Know

Using the knowledge that you gained in your Learn and Assert work, you can brainstorm assertions aligned to your theme.

We often use a very basic technique: creating a list of stated premises. This practice literally crafts a list of statements about your theme, the proto-relationship map, and the proto-journey maps you just created. Note if any assertions are more likely to impact one or more specific personas.

You will end up with a simple list like this:

Starting assertion	Possible personas

We find that creating this list works best when you gather as a team. That may seem challenging because it is rare for team members to be in the same location to talk through the assertions and any questions. In the

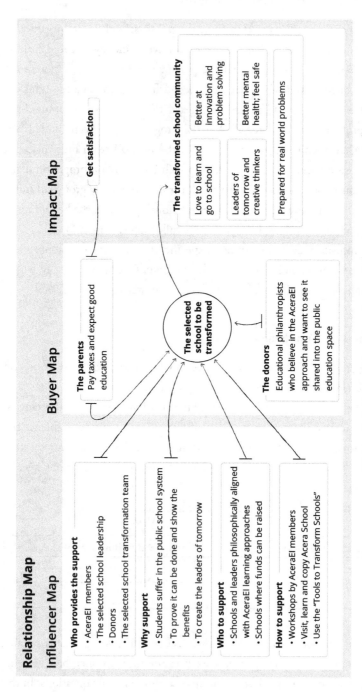

Figure 2.6 *AceraEI proto-relationship map*

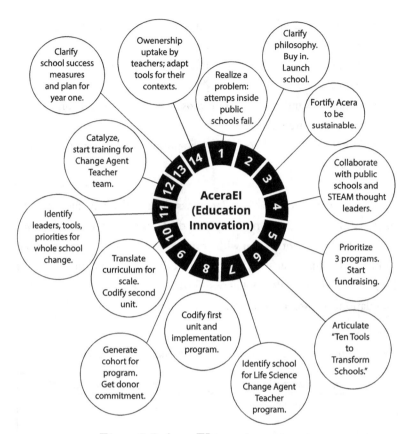

Figure 2.7 AceraEI proto-journey map

absence of sharing a space, you can easily accomplish this free-thinking activity using many tools built for basic collaboration. Consider trying Miro, Easyretro.io, Teams Whiteboard, or any other shared space that allows for open collaboration. When using one of these collaboration tools, just write down one assertion at a time on a sticky note or board. Then group the notes into categories.

Once you have decided on the brainstorming tool you will use, consider the following:

- What problems significantly or materially impact your customers or the industry as aligned to this theme?

- What are the lifecycles (product, service, process, and so on) related to the theme?
- What issues does each persona have within the context of your theme?
- What does influence mean to those who have the issue or those who are impacted?
- What else do you know about the problem you are trying to solve?

Don't worry, we have amazing news. You will likely disprove the majority of what you assume. Why does the Compassion-Driven Innovation methodology bother you with creating something you are just going to break? Because you need to set a stake in the ground that provides insight into what you do not know and what you need to learn. With that foundation, you are ready to learn, evaluate, and pivot to better solutions.

Example of Write What You Know for Innovation: Africa

Starting assertion	Possible personas
Villagers would like clean water and an electricity-powered pump to bring them the clean water.	Villagers
To get access to electricity, a solution to generating energy is needed. It has to be simple, sustainable, and cost-free to the villagers. Solar energy is free and available most of the year in Africa. Installing solar panels can generate the energy that is needed.	Electrician Engineer
A village may want water for agriculture in addition to drinking water.	Villagers
To provide enough clean water for a village, it is not enough to have just a pump; to plan for fluctuations in demand and supply, you must have a way to store the water. A water tower may be an option.	Civil Engineer Water Engineer
Many people with different skills will be required to complete each project.	Innovation: Africa CEO

A dedicated team of leaders needs to be assigned to work on a project.	Innovation: Africa Country Director, Deputy Country Director
Getting approval or buy-in from the whole community of the village is essential before starting any effort.	Innovation: Africa local Africa team and Innovation: Africa staff
Local and regional government buy-in will be critical to the approval of helping any villages, especially as Innovation: Africa will be acting as a nongovernmental and nonprofit organization providing water and electricity.	Minister of Water Minister of Health Minister of Energy District officers Village chiefs
The maintenance to replace parts or fix any problems needs to be done by the local employees or villagers.	Local trained employees or villagers
A dedicated local group needs to be created in every village to take responsibility for managing the maintenance and communication with Innovation: Africa.	Village Solar Committee

Example of Write What You Know for Gutter Tex

Starting assertion	Possible personas
Homeowners wish to have in-person contact during the quote, approval, and installation process.	Homeowner
Salespeople must talk to customers to get a customer to want to buy from their organizations.	Salesperson, homeowner
Salespeople can close more deals when they have a positive relationship and in-person contact with homeowners.	Salesperson, homeowner, installation engineer, chief operating officer
Concrete used in many foundations expands and shrinks, so if you do not have gutters, the water runoff from the roof will ruin the concrete slabs that are typical foundations in the Austin, Texas area.	Homeowners, installation engineer, salesperson, marketing
Homeowners decide that they need new gutters when existing gutters are pulling away from their home or sagging.	Homeowners, neighbors

Homeowners determine that they need first-time gutters on their home when they see damage in their landscaping.	Homeowners, marketing
Asphalt roofs cause toxic runoff, so if you do not have gutters, your garden and the safety of your vegetable gardens will be compromised.	Homeowner
Gutter Tex has a high-quality product and installation technique that differentiates them from other companies.	Homeowner, Salesperson, installation engineer, marketing, chief operating officer
To provide an accurate quote, a salesperson from Gutter Tex needs to manually inspect the house.	Salesperson, installation engineer, chief operating officer
To make an accurate parts order list, the salesperson must create a drawing that indicates the locations of the gutters, the length and height of each placement location, and indicate any incidental activities that must also occur (for example: Repair rotted materials; remove existing gutters).	Salesperson, installation engineer, chief operating officer

Example of Write What You Know for AceraEI

Starting assertion	Possible personas
It is possible for children to love school because they love to learn. School should be a refuge for students.	Students, AceraEI change agent teacher team
Students will thrive where they can learn based upon their abilities, needs and interests, without limits due to their age or to curriculum norms and standards.	Students, AceraEI change agent teacher team, Selected School Transformation team
Schools should help students develop core capacities, rather than teaching them to do well on tests. Examples of these capacities are systems thinking, creativity, emotional intelligence, perspective taking, critical thinking, problem-solving, ethical decision making, collaboration, and leadership. We need to normalize new ways to assess schoolwide success and hold ourselves accountable for more than standardized test scores.	Students, AceraEI change agent teacher team, selected school transformation team

Starting assertion	Possible personas
Schools would best serve society if they were places where students could learn to see needs, ideate solutions, and engage in their communities.	Students, AceraEI change agent teacher team
Teaching methods can impact a child's ability to innovate and solve problems.	Students, AceraEI change agent teacher team
Learning will be most relevant, meaningful, motivating, and durable when it is connected to real-world needs and put into a contextual framework around topics that matter to students and give them a sense of purpose.	Students, AceraEI change agent teacher team
Schools often have standard operating procedures and habits which can harm students, exacerbate the mounting issues of anxiety and depression, and squelch students' innate curiosity. We need instead to transition to school cultures and pedagogical norms which are backed by evidence of how young people learn and develop optimally for positive self-concept to set them up for success as adults.	Students, AceraEI change agent teacher team
Public school teachers want to do what is best for their students and want help to improve their teaching practice.	AceraEI change agent teacher team, parents, teachers
Public schools can change by making the school day engaging, fun, meaningful, and a place to belong through relationships with teachers, each other, and high interest hands-on and interdisciplinary discussion, projects, and work.	Selected school leadership and transformation team

As you can see from the examples, the types of assertions and the way in which you represent them will vary widely between projects. You can use these as tools to understand your project in ways that are meaningful to you.

Prioritize

If you are working with exceptional collaborators such as those involved in our case studies, you will likely create more assertions than can be analyzed in a specified timeframe.

Model innovators[11] use focus to drive both organizational and innovation success. Create focus by using your theme as a guardrail. Are there assertions or even entire categories of assertions that you can deprioritize that do not align to your theme? Before you go to the next step, spend time reducing your list to a manageable number of assertions. We recommend no more than 20.

Learn to Let Go

The maps and assertions you initially create are not meant to be permanent. They are a starting point in gathering feedback. If you find yourself or your teammates clinging to an assertion or theory, you must examine why. Is it truth or is it opinion? Few things cause innovation to go off track faster than unchecked dogma.

If you get attached to an idea, you are likely to consciously or unconsciously align findings to support the idea. True innovation must continually question ideas. It is not in our nature to doubt our understanding and try to see new trends in data. But to leapfrog and find new paths, we must do exactly that.

Have no fear. You will note that we talk in terms of *prioritizing*, not in terms of *throwing away*. We do not doubt that if you are following the methodology so far, you will generate brilliant ideas and theories. Some of these may not align to this specific project at this point in time. Keep a list of deprioritized items. A lot can change in six months or a year. You can always reevaluate the ideas in a new project when the timeframe or technology shifts. What may seem improbable one month may very well be likely in the next.

---

[11] S. Kirsner. November 29, 2019. "What Companies that are Good at Innovation Get Right." *Harvard Business Review.* https://hbr.org/2019/11/what-companies-that-are-good-at-innovation-get-right

Activity: Put Assert Into Action

☐ Identify the proto-personas.
☐ Create proto-relationship maps.
☐ Create proto-journey maps.
☐ Write what you know.

Now that you know your assertions, you are ready to move into the Discover stage.

Stage 2: Discover

Introduction to the Discover Stage

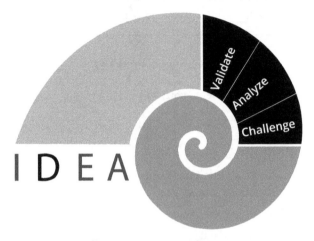

Figure 3.1 The Discover stage

The Discover (D) stage (Figure 3.1) requires curiosity about and compassion for the problems of buyers and users of the potential innovation. The assertion that great innovation requires deep empathy is not new; the role of customer empathy in project success is well-studied and widely documented.[1] The Compassion-Driven Innovation methodology takes empathy (a feeling) a step farther to compassion, invoking a cognitive desire to help solve the problems of the subject (an action). In this stage, you will:

- Use the assertions from the Include stage to create unbiased questions.
- Conduct interviews to uncover the *real* challenges you need to solve.
- Reassess the maps and journeys to unearth the unknown with ruthless detachment from your opinions and ideas.

---

[1] Kolko, J. November 20, 2014. "For Any Product to Be Successful, Empathy is Key." *Harvard Business Review*. https://hbr.org/2014/11/for-any-product-to-be-successful-empathy-is-key

The two outputs of this stage are as follows:

- A refined understanding of the customer journey.
- Identification of points of friction to be solved.

These two areas offer the best opportunities for innovation.

Discover Checklist

Following are the steps you will take in this stage of the methodology:

- ☐ Validate your understanding.
  - ☐ Develop nonleading questions.
  - ☐ Script your interviews.
  - ☐ Conduct outreach.
- ☐ Analyze the data.
  - ☐ Generate new maps.
  - ☐ Revisit personas to do a bottoms-up validation of your findings.
- ☐ Understand the challenges.
  - ☐ Create challenge maps.
  - ☐ Spin out challenges and projects.

The next section depicts a real-world example of using this checklist in the Discover stage.

Example of Imagine Innovation: Africa's Discover Stage

How would you approach this stage in the Innovation: Africa journey? Jot down some notes and compare them to ours: Using your best guesses about how to solve the problems you have found based on the secondary research and input from locals on your extended team, you visit multiple villages. There, you interview and shadow villagers to refine your understanding of the daily problems they face. You also search for any underlying preconditions or problems that must be solved to enable resolution of the broader problems. Once you have analyzed the data, you prioritize the most pressing problems and create a current state visual representation, or journey map. This map highlights several life-threatening situations: no clean water for drinking, cooking, and bathing; scarce medical treatment because there is no refrigerator for medications. Without medications, doctors focus their time elsewhere. Children and adults are malnourished. And many children are not in school learning, which means that little hope exists of changing their condition.

Validate Your Understanding

Your goal for the validation step is to gain an unbiased qualitative understanding of how the people in your persona or buyer map see their journey and their biggest challenges within your theme. You recognize and remediate personal bias in this step by crafting nonleading questions. You remediate customer bias by interviewing a variety of people representing different personas. By performing validation using process, scripts, and compassion, you will get a solid set of information that clearly identifies challenges to solve and opportunities for innovation.

Validation and interviewing techniques are widely studied across many academic programs and written about by User Experience[2] and Agile process experts.[3] We cover only the minimum viable efforts that we have found work best for us. This is not the only process that exists, nor is it the most thorough. If this section interests you, consider searching for advanced techniques involving User Experience customer interviews.

---

[2] P. Thornton. March 02, 2019. "How to Conduct User Interviews." *UX Collective.* https://uxdesign.cc/how-to-conduct-user-interviews-fe4b8c34b0b7
[3] S. Mansour. 2021. "Turning info into insights with the Customer Interview Pyramid." *ATLASSIAN Agile Coach.* www.atlassian.com/agile/design/product-design-process-customer-interview (accessed April 24, 2021).

Develop Nonleading Questions

Be forewarned: The first time you try to craft a series of nonleading questions, you may feel like you are trying to nail gelatin to a wall. The questions will seem to lack the consistency to stay put or to drive any meaningful insights. Many of us want to make our questions incredibly specific to ensure we get the data we need. However, you need to trust that there are things undiscovered that are as important as what you think you want to know.

All you need to do in this section is to form open-ended questions that could disprove or prove a starting assertion. Remember this: You already created a list. You documented your team's assertions. You identified some personas. You will now form questions to prove or disprove them.

For each list item, determine whether each starting assertion the team made is fact or hypothesis. For example: One assertion we could use in Gutter Tex is, "A salesperson will have access to a personal device while assessing a home." This is a fact we can prove through equipment assessment, whereas a statement such as, "Homeowners want salespeople to send real time quotes" is a hypothesis. You do not need to create questions for facts.

The following is an example you can use to create your list of questions by persona:

Starting assertion	Personas	Question to disprove this	Segment, if applicable

Note that we use the existing "Starting Assertion" and "Personas" columns and add in "Questions to disprove this" and "Segment, if applicable." If you are working on a business challenge, in addition to personas, you may also have vertical differentiation. Are there different theoretical answers by persona or vertical based on the state-of-the-art research? Consider whether you need to look at different industries, company sizes, geographies, or other typical variants.

For each list item, create at least one open-ended question to ask each of the listed personas. An open-ended question is one that invites explanation. For example, "What do you think about food trucks?" Your question should not discourage the interviewee from sharing, which would happen with a "yes" or "no" question, such as, "Do you like food trucks?" You also should avoid leading questions, such as, "You think food trucks are great, right?" Asking questions that lead to dead ends is the opposite of what we want to do.

Resist the temptation to frame questions that lead your interviewees to tell you what they think you want to hear. Don't worry that others may think you are poorly informed if you do not show your knowledge and prowess. Save that for later. Right now, your job is to invite interviewees to tell their stories so you can understand their perspectives outside of the influence of your bias. Open-ended questions that do not box in responses do not reflect poorly on you. On the contrary, seeking to understand others' points of view takes courage—the courage to venture to where you may not be an expert or have all the answers if you are asked.

This is easily understood through examples.

Example of Innovation: Africa Questions

As part of validating the assertions, a team from Innovation: Africa is assigned to visit the village, create a report about the condition of the village, and include recorded testimonies to provide Sivan all the information she needs to decide whether or not to invest in this village. The report also includes details about how to help the village.

As we are highlighting the work of Innovation: Africa after they have invested decades in their compassion-driven approach, we have the benefit of hindsight to highlight why this step is so important.

By January 2009, Innovation: Africa had completed four projects in Tanzania. In these projects, they installed solar panels in four villages. When they returned to see how the installations had impacted the villages, they were met with a challenge.

In Sivan's words, "I went back to check that everything's okay, and then I realized that no one was using solar energy. It took me time [to find out what had happened], but they told me that the witches in the villages are not approving of solar energy, because they are saying that it

takes away their powers. Further, they prohibited children from going to the school where the panels were located."

After this incident, the solar panels were removed from these villages and were installed in others. In response, the Innovation: Africa team added nonleading questions to the report checklist to validate that no one in the village in a position of perceived authority objected to installing solar panels and using their energy.

Given differences in culture, this example is also an exceptional way to highlight the dangers of leading questions. Imagine you asked a village member, "Wouldn't you be happy if we brought you clean water?" Unwritten cultural norms may dictate that it is impolite to contradict a visitor. Instead, we need to ask open-ended questions that aim to understand the needs of the community.

For the sake of brevity, we highlight in the following table a few assertions about how to choose a village and understand villagers' needs most effectively.

Starting assertion	Personas	Question to disprove this	Segment, if applicable
All villages would like clean electricity and an electricity-powered pump to bring them clean water.	Village members	Have you or members of your community used electricity in the past? Solar electricity? What was the reaction to the technology? Please describe any reasons against using electricity.	By region, village
A village may need access to water for agriculture.	Village members, Village leaders	Please describe the ways your village would like to use water. Please describe your village food sources. What techniques are used for creating food? Are there any challenges? Please describe your ideal situation for self-sustainable food.	By region, village, job (such as farmer versus a baker or other role)

Example of Gutter Tex Questions

In the example of Gutter Tex, as we review the major changes that have happened over the last five years in their business, we find that they discovered ways to innovate within the customer interaction and installation process itself. Where many business owners may have simply optimized routes for efficiency and cost reduction, Daniel was able to consider what different people needed throughout the journey and challenge some of the most fundamental assumptions in the home repairs industry. He rethought everything from face-to-face customer interactions to eliminating high pressure sales and realized that internal relationships were as critical as external ones.

Imagining where they started, we find that he challenged a basic assertion that homeowners desired to be present when a quote was completed. Following we show the examples around that theme.

Starting assertion	Personas	Question to disprove this	Segment, if applicable
To provide an accurate quote, a salesperson from Gutter Tex needs to manually inspect the house.	Salesperson, installation engineer, Chief Operating Officer	What aspects of a building need to be understood to provide a quote within 10% accuracy? What are the different ways one could get the measurements of a building?	Residential, business/commercial buildings, municipal buildings
Homeowners wish to have in-person contact during the quote, approval, and installation process.	Homeowner	Please describe the process you used to make your last major purchase over $1,000. What did you think of the process? Were there any ways it could have been more efficient? Please tell me about the best ordering and service experience you have had in the last several years? Please explain the process you engaged in. Please describe your ideal gutter-buying experience.	Residential

Example of AceraEI Questions

The Assert step for AceraEI theorized that children were not doing well in school due to outmoded teaching practices and an emphasis on rote memory. The AceraEI team believed that developing core capacities and habits for thinking, creativity, and initiative would better serve students. How can we craft questions that could disprove that statement? Some people would approach it directly by asking a parent, "Do your children feel unhappy in school because there is too much time spent on lectures, passive listening, and test-based teaching?" Do you see anything problematic with this question? This is called a leading question, and it is exactly the type of question you need to avoid. It implies an answer in the question itself and closes interviewees off from sharing because they will likely answer "yes" or "no." This is the opposite of what we want to do. Instead, ask open-ended questions and move from general to specific topics.

Notice that each of the questions is open-ended, inviting further conversation. In this example, you create general awareness by understanding the larger challenges. This is often where you will find that you can group personas into buyer groupings. You create situational awareness by homing in on the theme challenges. You then create specific awareness by asking an open-ended question about the topic of interest.

Starting assertion	Personas	Question to disprove this	Segment, if applicable
Public school teachers *want* to do what is best for their students and welcome help to improve their teaching practice.	Public school leaders, teachers	What are the biggest challenges your students face in general? What are the biggest challenges your students face in relation to schooling? What is not working in your school? What outcomes/results for students would you like instead?	Middle school, grammar school, high school, district

Starting assertion	Personas	Question to disprove this	Segment, if applicable
Parents of children who are suffering in the public school system are looking for education options that support development of students' core capacities.	Parents, students	Please describe your ideal experience for your child's schooling. Please describe your current experience with your child's schooling. What options have you considered for closing the gap between the two?	New vertical may occur due to cultures.

Script Your Interviews

Your list with questions needs to be turned into one interview script for each persona-type you will interview. We put the questions into a chart so that you can organize by persona the questions you already created. (Many questions will appear on more than one script.) Voila! You have the baseline for your interview scripts. You are almost done.

Brace yourself. We apologize for a small, benign deception. Now that you have a script, you will need to break the "no leading questions" rule and create anchor questions. An anchor question is a "yes," "no," or multiple choice answer that gives you a clear statistical understanding of one aspect of your interview. This question will be used to match different open-ended questions against each other.

Using our previous example for AceraEI, we crafted a script for a proto-persona of "parent of middle school kid." To make the script and interview answers *analyzable*, we add the anchor question in bold:

- What are the biggest challenges your students face in general?
- What are the biggest challenges your students face in relation to schooling?
- What is not working in your school?
- What outcomes/results for students would you like instead?

- Can you describe any one or thing that may resist changing the way students currently learn in school?
- Do you believe that children are succeeding in school? [anchor question]

Why break the nonleading rule? At its simplest, we figured out that it is too difficult to collate answers if you *do not* break the rule at least once in an interview. After performing interviews, you use the anchor questions to collate answers. In our example, asking this straightforward question helps us create groupings to see if parents of students they perceive as succeeding have different perspectives than parents who do not.

Once you add anchor questions, you have interview scripts. Make sure the whole team has the opportunity to review the personas and scripts. Ask for feedback: Are any of the questions difficult to understand? Do any seem irrelevant? Did you miss any critical areas for understanding? As part of the review process, consider the different ways you can synthesize output. Make sure you are asking the questions that would enable you to generate the types of charts, maps, and other data that you will want when you communicate the output and formulate the next round of inputs.

Find the Resisters

Within each script, you will want to add one or more questions which ask if the person is aware of anyone who may resist change within the context of the theme you are discussing.

In the AceraEI example, we capture this with the question: "Can you describe anyone or anything that may resist changing the way students are currently taught in school?"

You may think that the question is too broad. An important principle of Compassion-Driven Innovation is an awareness of *all* people impacted by your theme. Not everyone will be in favor of changing the way things are. Consider those who may be forced to modify their behavior or who could lose their jobs if a challenge is solved. You can be sure innovation that results in job loss will be met with resistance. If you disregard the people who may challenge your desire to change the status quo, you will be unprepared when they inevitably reject your proposal. Use this type of question to increase your situational awareness. If you can identify resistance up front, you may be able to innovate around it or add value to the resisters, too.

Choose Your Outreach Methods

It is tempting to use your scripts and jump right into interviewing people. Before you start pounding the virtual pavement looking for ideal interview candidates, consider the ways you can get feedback. Typical methods include the following:

- Written surveys
- Focus groups
- Social media posts/polls
- Product or website surveys
- Roundtables
- Ethnography
- Interviews.

This list is roughly ordered from lowest cost of effort to highest cost of effort.

Written Surveys

Written surveys are a low-cost method of gathering input. Surveys are useful when you are trying to get quantified feedback on easy-to-understand questions. Used properly, surveys can be a useful screening tool for high-level assertions. Your respondent's personal investment in a topic can impact the number and types of questions you can include in a survey. If you are sending a survey to a group who is very familiar with you or your organization and invested in your success, you can include a larger number of questions and more open-ended questions, which require written feedback. Survey tools often recommend keeping the survey to under five minutes of effort.

If you are sending the survey to a "cold" audience (people with whom you have not previously interacted) or people who have little to nothing

invested in completing the survey, you are going to want to keep it incredibly simple, short, and engaging. Some experts suggest no more than five questions.

Consider whether you are looking for qualitative or quantitative data. Surveys typically require a significant sample size to be considered quantifiable.

Focus Groups

Focus groups are effective for collecting data from a small number of people at the same time. To create a focus group, you determine how many people and which personas you would like to bring together for a discussion on a specific topic. You could select people who represent different personas within an industry or use case. This can provide real-time insights into how different personas interact. If you want a fast way to find commonalities among a single view, invite people who represent a single persona. These sessions are typically only an hour long, so plan your questions carefully.

Social Media Polls and Posts

Social outreach through personal or professional accounts is useful for engaging in short-term feedback. If you have a set of questions that can be crafted as yes/no or multiple choice options, consider opinion polls or social posts to solicit feedback on one topic or to get feedback on a specific question. Professional social networks can be useful for sharing or starting threads, which may lead to finding new people to talk to down the road. The danger of social networks is that they tend to create echo chambers: Users are likely to engage with similar thinkers, so you might not get diverse feedback. A second thing to be wary of is that many competitors stalk social accounts for insights and competitive data points.

Product or Website Prompts

Many websites support surveys. Prompting site or product visitors to answer questions through popups in your products or websites are great ways to engage your existing customer base in feedback. This can be a useful screening tool where you have a customer-specific audience in mind. This can, however, be challenging in larger organizations. If your team is not connected to the team running the website or deploying the product, you may have a difficult time getting your survey out. Consider this as you start to meet new people in your organization—who should or could you get to know that may make this type of customer engagement possible later?

Roundtables

Roundtables are an effective way to gather a group of customers or advisers together to provide directional feedback on ideas. In some cases, these roundtables are already occurring as part of marketing, sales, or product strategy projects. Consider if there are ways you can engage in existing roundtables. Could you ask for feedback from the team? Things to consider when engaging in roundtables are the "loudest voice syndrome" and groupthink. What can happen if you do not engage effectively is that one person will be the first or the loudest to speak, and other attendees may not feel comfortable raising dissenting opinions or ideas. In some cases, you can use online tools such as polls in real-time to get a first view of the opinions in the room and then follow that up with conversation about the reasons for the votes. This can be a more effective way of determining sentiment and achieving follow-up data.

Ethnography

Ethnography is a longer-term study, often written, which builds on a direct observation of users in their natural environment rather than in a laboratory. The objective of this type of research is to gain insights into how users interact with things in their natural environment, and it is of particular importance in innovation that impacts day-to-day lives. Ethnography is valuable in use cases such as Innovation: Africa, where it provides insights into village environments. It is also valuable in a case like that of AceraEI, in which observation can aid in identifying in-school behaviors.

Interviews

Nonleading conversations and interviews are a highly effective way of learning and gathering feedback. Given the growing use of video calls, we find that people are more comfortable engaging in remote one-on-one interviews. However, it is time-consuming. Consider the upfront cost of finding the people to interview, scheduling interviews, and the personnel time to host and then analyze the interviews.

Screening the interview candidates is essential to ensure that they meet the persona criteria and have the authority and responsibility needed to answer the questions. While you are recruiting, please take the time to double check that the people you recruit have the qualifications or responsibilities that meet your needs.

Consider conducting a "dry run" interview with a colleague to see how long the interview would likely take. Your interview length will depend on the time the interviewee has allotted to spend with you. We have conducted them for anywhere from 20 minutes to over an hour. Best practice is to have no more than four anchor questions and be prepared with 10 to 20 nonleading questions.

How to Conduct Interviews

If you haven't been professionally trained in conducting nonleading interviews, welcome to the club. Most of us haven't. It can be complicated, which is why we are including an extra section dedicated to this topic. The following are a few things to keep in mind so that you get from your interviewees honest perspectives that are untainted by your own biases.

With the interviewees' permission, record each interview and use a program or service to transcribe it. This enables you to focus on the interviewee instead of taking notes. You will use these transcripts in the Analyze stage.

Remember that your goal is to discover the perspectives of others. You can only do so by keeping your perspective to yourself. You can get more out of an interview by asking a teammate with a different perspective to participate in calls as an observer. This listener can text you questions to ask interviewees directly when answers are not clear. By having different perspectives on a call, you can improve the amount of data and insights you collect, reducing the need for follow-up conversations and of personal bias influencing the conversation and findings. When performing interviews, use the script as a starting point, and remember to follow up by asking "why."[4]

As more people work from home, remote interviews are becoming more common. Using video helps bridge that gap between voice-only and in-person interviews by enabling you to read body language and know when somebody needs help understanding your questions. Unfortunately, remote interviews also introduce technical difficulties, most of which can be avoided with a little proactive behavior. Simply log into meetings five minutes early, test your microphone and video and connection quality, and verify that you sent the right link to the attendee.

Empathize With Your Interviewee

Imagine you are the person who is about to take a survey, participate in a focus group, or be interviewed one-on-one. You likely are willing to share and teach within reasonable boundaries, but you also want your time and knowledge to be honored.

Interviewees may agree to take a survey, answer a poll, or have a conversation because they want to get something out of it. Perhaps their goal is to make a new connection or gain insight into an area. Maybe they have a pressing issue they are hoping someone will solve or they are getting paid for their time. Regardless of their motivations for participating, time from people is a gift.

Look for reciprocal opportunities for sharing, giving, and being grateful. Consider offering the participants a version of the findings so they can learn alongside you. Consider leaving five minutes at the end of a conversation and inviting the interviewee to ask you questions. These interactions can be incredibly revealing and leave the interviewee with a

---

[4] The Five-Why technique was popularized by Sakichi Toyoda, who stated that "by repeating why five times, the nature of the problem as well as its solution becomes clear."

positive impression of the experience and your organization. It may even help create a more lasting connection.

End Interviews Graciously

On occasion, you will start an interview and realize that the person you are interviewing is either not able to answer your questions or not qualified to answer your questions. When this occurs, go off script and use the opportunity to learn what you can about what the person does and knows. Consider asking questions such as, "Can you describe some challenges in your current job/organization/during an activity of interest? Are you familiar with [insert an area of interest]? What does it mean to you?" You likely will be able to use this information as part of a future project, so consider this as an opportunity to collect data points for others who may go through state-of-the-art learning in the future. You do not have to use all the time scheduled or allotted.

On occasion, you will interview someone who was a paid participant recruited by an outside organization. If they do not meet your requirements, politely ask a few qualifying questions to verify whether they have the qualifying skills or attributes which were requested when recruiting. Thank them for their time and graciously end the call. Follow up offline with the recruiting agency with a record of the disconnect between the requirements and the skill set.

Regardless of whom you interview, one of the best ways to end the interview is to ask if there is anything that the interviewee thinks you should have asked or would like you to know. This is a great way to help the interviewee feel listened to and typically results in learning something unique and interesting.

Summary

Think through the types of engagements you can pursue and look at your existing question set. Can some questions be easily answered with low-cost, low-effort outreach? Are there basic questions that could prove or disprove a theory? Prioritize those questions. Is there a lower cost way to find those answers efficiently, such as a short survey to gather feedback quickly?

A word of caution: Always follow your organization's guidelines when doing primary research. Reaching out to customers could be deemed a breach of privacy or a "do not contact" agreement. Interviewing some respondents may require nondisclosure agreements, or your organization may have other branding or rule restrictions. Also be sure you understand your company's data protection and privacy policies for storing information. For example, if you record interviews that contain protected information that identifies the source, you will want guidance from your legal or privacy team about requirements for labeling and storing that data.

Use a Recruitment Process

Innovation teams frequently either fail to reach adequate numbers of people or access the "wrong" people. We see this happen for three main reasons: a lack of clarity, a lack of contacts, or a lack of comfort.

Those who lack clarity often cast a vague email into their contacts or sales teams asking for customer names or interviews. The innovation team members are disappointed when the sales teams do not reply with a hundred candidates lined up.

Consider why sales representatives may hesitate to bring you their customer list. They succeed by creating personal relationships. They give generously to the customer.[5] When you ask a sales representative to get something *from* the customer, such as an interview, you are potentially tipping the balance of the relationship. If you want representatives to put this balance on the line, you must provide clarity and purpose in your communications and requests. And you need to find a way to have the conversation provide value to the customer.

Innovation teams that lack contacts may send surveys or schedule calls with existing, known friendly contacts who make them comfortable. If you repeatedly interview the same people, ask yourself whether you are doing so out of convenience. Figure out what is holding you back. You may need to consider how you are finding and recruiting people to interview. We have great luck finding people through LinkedIn. However, if comfort

---

[5] Ferrazzi, K. July 11, 2012. "How to Turn a Relationship Into a Sale." *Harvard Business Review.* https://hbr.org/2012/07/how-to-turn-a-relationship-int

is the challenge and recruiting is not your strong suit, consider working with a professional recruiter. Professional researchers and other third parties have the skills and contacts to set up basic and advanced research outreach. This can save you significant time if you are not well-connected.

If you still fail to contact the right people, you may be missing one key ingredient—a process. Relationship managers already know this: Success in recruiting is greatly increased when you create focus and allocate time and energy to finding contacts.

You have your interview question list, which includes personas and segment breakouts. Decide how many people you want to interview, survey, or otherwise engage with for each persona and category. Create a spreadsheet that includes a company name, the contact name (if you have it), the persona they represent, email, last contact attempt, and the current status to track your outreach.

Now simply pursue your list. Some ways to do this include the following:

- Post your list.
- Send your list to people who can help.
- Find people through social media.
- Attend organization meetings.
- Ask for referrals.

Share the spreadsheet and interview scripts with your colleagues and ask for specific recruiting help. Track their outreach and recruit interviewees on your own. Tracking enables you to ask for help from more people when you know you are in trouble. If you are not keeping records, you will be challenged to define success and get help before you fail.

Before you engage in high-commitment activities such as interviews or round tables, we encourage you to screen (or validate) the interview candidates to be sure they have expertise in the area of focus. Screening can be done with a few simple questions and save significant time and awkwardness. Verify things such as job titles, age, responsibilities and, if there are areas of expertise, one or two qualifying questions.

How many contacts you complete depends on the size and scope of your project. In the industries we have covered, we can typically discover a trend in a single persona from six to eight conversations. If you are aiming at a single persona and a limited number of segments, this is probably a rational number.

We recommend creating outreach plans that support two rounds of learning. In one example, our team wanted to speak with one persona in one industry. We recruited eight people to get an understanding of a well-scoped theme and set of hypotheses. We discovered new segments from the first round of conversations. We then revised our scripts, updated our outreach list, and added another persona. We had a well-scoped set of hypotheses and questions which we verified with an additional round of six to eight highly qualified candidates.

Get Help

If you are unable to conduct outreach, surveys, or interviews, or if you lack the time, skill, or resources to run the interviews yourself, professional research organizations can assist with research at all levels. In many large organizations, this task is frequently outsourced.

Consider hiring professional researchers to help if your team needs skill augmentation or resources to scale. If you go this route, conduct a few interviews yourself to make sure the scripts or surveys are well-composed and net the results you expect. Participate in the interviews as much as possible alongside the researcher to help further develop empathy for the interviewees.

Activity: Put Validate into Action

☐ Develop nonleading questions.
☐ Script your interviews.
☐ Create your interviewee spreadsheet.
☐ Determine who and how many people you will contact.
☐ Conduct outreach.
☐ Perform interviews, send surveys, and collect responses.

Regardless of whether you hire outside interview firms or perform the interviews and surveys yourself, you must turn the data into knowledge. The next step will help you achieve this by synthesizing the information into a few different views.

Analyze Data

In the Analyze Data step, you will synthesize the data you collected by generating new maps, identifying bottom-up personas to create for validation, and assessing whether qualitative validation is required.

Generate New Maps

Recall the proto-relationship map from the Include stage. The map is a visual representation of all of the people who could be influential or directly included or impacted by the innovation. You now have enough data to draw a *real* relationship map. Additionally, you will now use the interview data to create a *real* journey map.

By drawing out the map and creating flows, you may start to see gaps in information. Challenges and inefficiencies may become clearer. When you visualize the other personas whom each interviewee thinks are in their journey, you may find similarities or differences between the people you talk to. This will give you new ways of segmenting customers and buyers.

Use the new drawings you have for the relationship maps and journey maps as input to create a single all-inclusive version. Look for patterns. Work to create a single journey map that represents all the interviews accurately. You may discover that you need to create different journey maps for groups that align to the anchor question answers. Did new groups emerge? Identifying patterns enables more efficient problem solving as you enter later Compassion-Driven Innovation stages.

As you start to combine multiple customers into a single journey, the circular way of conveying a journey may no longer fit your needs. You may find that you run out of space. You can transition your map into a linear journey map (Figure 3.2).

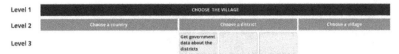

Figure 3.2 Example linear journey map

This is a way of visualizing a process from left to right. You have a row at the top which expresses a high-level grouping (Level 1). The second row shows subgroupings (Level 2). The third row should detail the steps within the subgrouping (Level 3), and so on.

At the end of this practice, you will have a set of relationship and journey maps with a reasonable understanding of who is impacted by your theme and how they are impacted.

Example of the Analyze Data Step for Innovation: Africa

Innovation: Africa used an interesting method of data gathering called ethnography. In this type of research, a team member traveled to locations to gather data. They determined the types of support that each village they visited needed. They were also able to determine whether there were any obstacles within the village—including any people who may object to this support. After gathering this information, they used it to determine which villages should be supported and the order in which they should support them.

In the Analyze example, you can see some of the detailed data analysis. In this image, we zoom into Level 3 in the journey. This column shows the data gathered from the government to understand where to operate in the country. They need to choose a village (Level 1). However, to do that, they need to select regions (Level 2). Then, where possible, the CEO of Innovation: Africa, the County Director, and the Deputy County Director gather data about the regions so they can decide where to operate within the country (Level 3). In the next project, when Innovation: Africa starts in a new country, they can follow the journey map to be sure they complete all the steps (Figure 3.3).

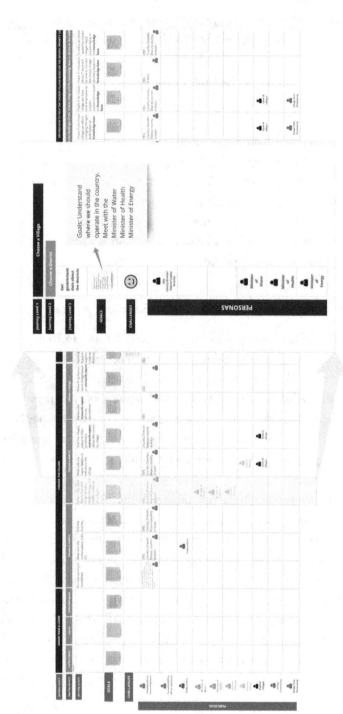

Figure 3.3 Example journey map for Innovation: Africa

Example of the Analyze Data Step for Gutter Tex

Over the years, Daniel has honed his craftsmanship and people skills by working his way up through millwork on high-end homes to co-owning his business. He has done every job in the value chain for his business at some point, from sales to installation, giving him a great understanding of and respect for his employees' skills. As a homeowner and friend, he saw the pain that poor contractor practices could inflict on good people. With this experience, he dedicated himself to being the kind of business owner who cares deeply for his employees and his customers. He set the bar to ensure high-quality work and satisfied customers over easy profit.

When considering what it means to have happy customers, Daniel realized that many homeowners were not comfortable having salespeople in their homes or discussing the specifics of construction-type projects because they are not experts in this area. They simply want their problems solved. Similarly, from a salesperson perspective, he realized that spending time in a stranger's home could also feel uncomfortable, particularly if the homeowner is projecting discomfort. He realized that with access to home data prior to a visit, he could make the process more efficient and more pleasant; and with a high-quality product and a great reputation, he knew he could set fair pricing and remove high-pressure sales techniques.

With this perspective, we will zoom into what Daniel discovered in the "Choose Provider" portion of his customer journey (Figure 3.4).

In this case, the simple step which was initially thought to be "Choose Provider" is actually a few steps. First is the process of scheduling quotes, followed by the process of choosing a vendor. And within the scheduling quotes process, there are actually three steps that a homeowner has to do:

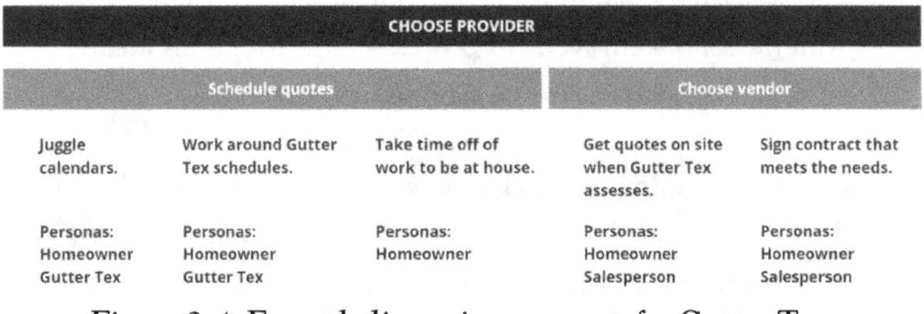

CHOOSE PROVIDER				
Schedule quotes			Choose vendor	
Juggle calendars.	Work around Gutter Tex schedules.	Take time off of work to be at house.	Get quotes on site when Gutter Tex assesses.	Sign contract that meets the needs.
Personas: Homeowner Gutter Tex	Personas: Homeowner Gutter Tex	Personas: Homeowner	Personas: Homeowner Salesperson	Personas: Homeowner Salesperson

Figure 3.4 Example linear journey map for Gutter Tex

- Make time in their calendar to set up quotes.
- Work around a vendor schedule.
- Take time off from work to be present when a vendor arrives.

This kind of illustration is critical for revealing the many actions that go into each high-level journey. We will want to use this information to our advantage in the next step.

Example of the Analyze Data Step for AceraEI

As Acera School engaged with students who were exceptionally talented—but who had struggled with public school teaching methods—its faculty and staff built and tested their novel curriculum step-by-step on a shoestring budget. Seeing their methods unlock sophisticated thinking and a passion for learning, Courtney's team created "Tools to Transform Schools." Empowered with this toolkit, the members of the AceraEI outreach program could begin taking what they had discovered to public schools nearby. This was the next step toward the vision of transforming public schools across the nation.

One of the top-level steps validated in the journey for AceraEI was this decision to transform a public school. As illustrated in Figure 3.5, the data supported four subactions within this major step. These are considered the Level 2 actions.

The subactions that appear in Level 2 under the step "Transform a Public School" are as follows:

- Engage with the public school.
- Conduct a workshop with the district leaders and principals.
- Perform school planning and conduct a staff workshop.
- Run the school engagement process—prioritize tools, define success, pilot, conduct workshops, engage and assess.

Zooming in within the Level 2 substep "Perform School Planning," AceraEI research revealed that a public school was unable to adopt wholesale change for many reasons. This finding in the Discovery stage helped the AceraEI team to understand that—although all 10 "Tools to Transform

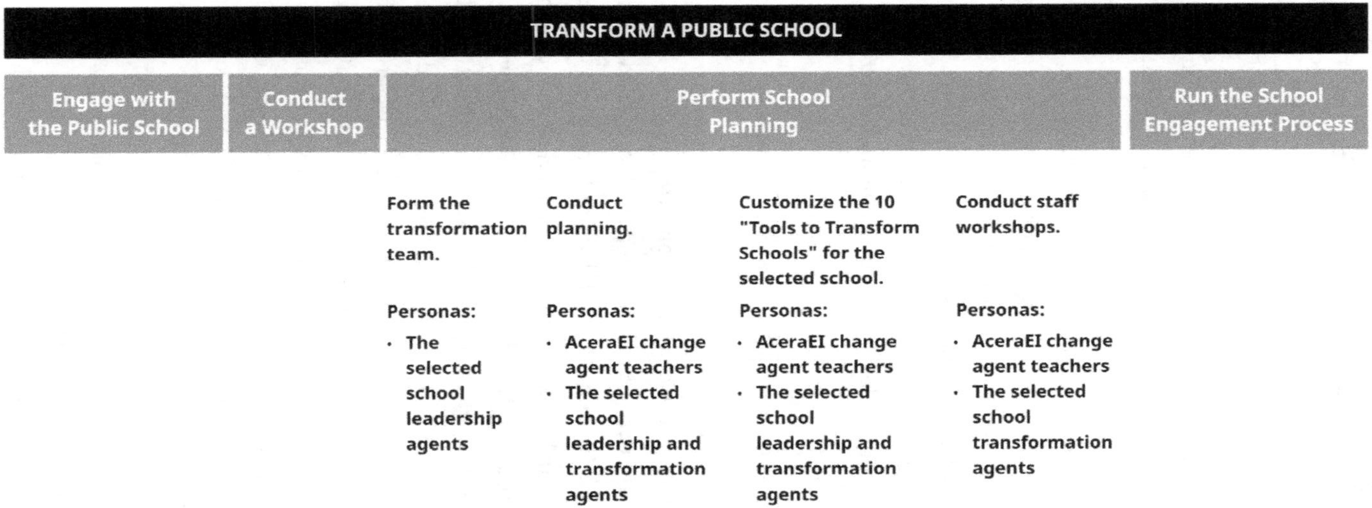

TRANSFORM A PUBLIC SCHOOL

Engage with the Public School	Conduct a Workshop	Perform School Planning	Run the School Engagement Process
Form the transformation team.	Conduct planning.	Customize the 10 "Tools to Transform Schools" for the selected school.	Conduct staff workshops.
Personas:	Personas:	Personas:	Personas:
· The selected school leadership agents	· AceraEI change agent teachers · The selected school leadership and transformation agents	· AceraEI change agent teachers · The selected school leadership and transformation agents	· AceraEI change agent teachers · The selected school transformation agents

Figure 3.5 Example journey map for AceraEI

Schools" are used with great success within the Acera School—a public school must generate momentum one tool at a time.

Summary

Using a journey map as a tool helps to visualize the research findings in a way that can reveal hidden aspects and challenges—such as emotions, cultural differences, and resistance to change which can dramatically affect the project's future existence. These are usually seen as nontechnical problems, so they are easily disregarded by teams working on the innovative solution. Successfully transforming an organization such as a public school system that for decades used the same methods and philosophy can be done when we reveal these challenges and innovate to overcome them using the Compassion-Driven Innovation methodology.

Revisiting Personas to do a Bottoms-Up Validation of Your Findings

Performing separate persona validation research is a luxury afforded to those who have deep teams and a lot of time. Should you have both, we recommend a "bottoms-up" validation of the personas you generate by sending a researcher with fresh eyes to interview people who represent each persona. You can provide the persona researcher with the work to date or have them craft their interview scripts without the data you've gathered. Using a secondary researcher will help you discover whether your maps and journeys are verifiable by another style of research.

When the persona researcher returns with the data and completed persona work, review the work together. Note any areas that may conflict with your findings. Your goal here is to find flaws in your maps or journeys. Did you misunderstand something? Should you be aware of a new market or persona segment and make different decisions based on that knowledge? Present your version of the innovation findings to the persona researcher. What notes do they have? Are there areas that do not match with their findings or opinions?

We have used this method to successfully identify additional holes or friction points in customer journeys. We have also used it to deepen the discovery of key technologies or messaging that must be considered in the innovation. If you have identified major disconnects or shifts in findings, you may need to revisit validation and gather additional nonleading feedback. The first time you go through this process, you may feel some despair. Just remember that pivoting in the Discover stage and reassessing your project will result in significant time and cost savings versus failing when you go to market with a product or service that misses the mark.

Rinse and Repeat

You may need to repeat validation and analysis if your interviews produce a radical shift in thinking. It is not unusual for discoveries in the initial round of interviews to result in completely rewriting an interview script or even spinning out a new project.

Activity: Put Analyze Data into Action

- ☐ Generate a new relationship map.
- ☐ Generate a collective journey map.
- ☐ Revisit personas to do a bottoms-up validation of your findings.
- ☐ Assess whether qualitative validation is required.

Now that we have performed a baseline analysis, we will explore how to call attention to the challenges.

Understand the Challenges

A wise salesperson once said that it does not matter what you build; if it does not solve a problem or get a company more customers, no one will ever buy it. And Einstein is attributed with saying that your ability to solve a problem is directly correlated to how well you define it. We agree with both. And therefore, we need clearly defined problems to solve that are meaningful to our target customers.

Compassion-Driven Innovation uses the Challenge step to bring focus to areas within your theme that may benefit the most from innovation or which may be effective ways to express the value of your innovation to potential buyers or users. Use this step to define your problems as specifically and honestly as you can using the interviews and research you have performed.

This step seems quite simple: Start with a virtual whiteboard or screen containing the journey maps. On a virtual sticky note or on the whiteboard, note where the interviewees perceived challenges in their journey, how frequent the challenges are, the severity the interviewees associated with the challenges, and the extent to which these challenges inhibit the personas. When you map challenges to the journey, try to attach them to the lower level of the journey. For example, if the journey has three levels describing the steps, try to map the challenges to Level 3. Do this by persona, by journey, and by any other segmentation that arose from your interviews.

While this step seems straightforward, be aware that you must balance two elements: empathy and precision. To empathize, you must stand in the shoes of the personas and imagine how they complete steps and what their experiences would feel like. To maintain precision in identifying pain points, you must check that your empathy can be *validated by the primary and secondary research.* You must avoid falling back to asserting beliefs in this step.

Remember to update the journey map as you learn new information, add journey steps, and capture new challenges. If you identify that steps are resolved over time (due to market or behavior changes), you should track what was fixed and update the journey. Having an outdated journey map may lead to avoidable mistakes.

Example of the Challenge Map for Innovation: Africa

In their first project, Innovation: Africa installed two solar panels to provide electricity to the clinic of a village in Tanzania. There was no doubt that this support would be lifesaving. However, when Sivan returned to the village to check the health status of the villagers, she found that many were still sick. The ill children were unable to attend school. Sivan's team traced the issue to the lack of access to clean water. Villagers were becoming ill from the water they drank. When Sivan examined the existing journey, she identified a challenge in how she decided to support each village based on its condition (Figure 3.6).

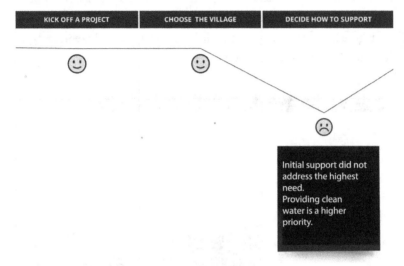

Figure 3.6 Challenge map for Innovation: Africa

Sivan could place a challenge sticky note in the Decide How to Support step.

Example of the Challenge Map for Gutter Tex

Daniel is dedicated to long-term internal and external relationships. He spends months training each new employee in the Gutter Tex process to ensure that each job is completed by highly skilled individuals trained in engineering and general home repairs. As a team, they recognize the value of time for homeowners, and that most homeowners are not fully comfortable with strangers in their home or on their property. To innovate, they had to consider how they could learn about the physical characteristics of a home to provide a fair estimate while minimizing disruption in the homeowners' day and building trust.

In calling into question many traditional service business customs such as face-to-face contact and requiring an adult to be home at the time

of quote, Gutter Tex completely transformed their operations and created a win–win situation for the sales team and customers. When we map the challenges into the newly updated journey, we can see that there were a series of Level 3 steps that put a great deal of burden on the homeowner. For example, homeowners are required to move their schedules around twice to accommodate both an initial quote and an initial meeting.

Figure 3.7 is an example of a Challenge map that only represents the Schedule Quotes Level 2 section.

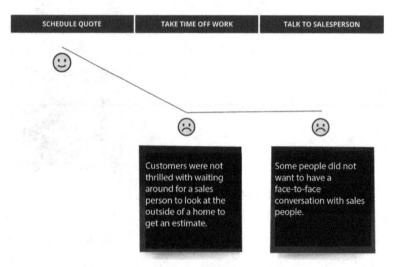

Figure 3.7 Challenge map for Gutter Tex

Example of the Challenge Map for AceraEI

When AceraEI was ready to take its innovative educational approach into public schools, the team faced multiple challenges. For this case study, we focus on one long-term challenge. Having grown organically and methodically, AceraEI lacked the resources to scale nationally. They had to begin by partnering with local schools to transform incrementally. To do so, the team formalized a Decide How to Transform step in which they helped public schools determine which of their 10 "Tools to Transform Schools" to adopt first (Figure 3.8).

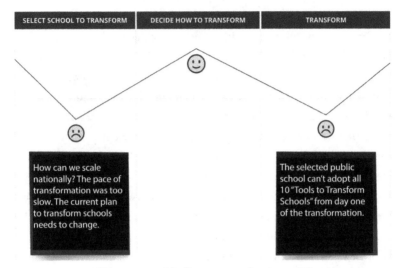

SELECT SCHOOL TO TRANSFORM   DECIDE HOW TO TRANSFORM   TRANSFORM

How can we scale nationally? The pace of transformation was too slow. The current plan to transform schools needs to change.

The selected public school can't adopt all 10 "Tools to Transform Schools" from day one of the transformation.

Figure 3.8 Challenge map for AceraEI

Summary

Order the challenges from most critical to least critical. Group them by persona. Do you start to see any trends in steps or journey areas that stand out as particularly painful? This is a great opportunity to ask for clarification if any challenges are not clear. You should take advantage of this step to cycle back and validate the challenges and ask clarifying questions if any of the issues are unclear.

To illustrate what can happen if you do not pay close attention to details, consider this example of a company that developed a software product requiring that end users install software in a specific location on their laptop: In user interviews, that requirement emerged as the home office users' single biggest challenge. Rather than acknowledging that the interviewees' opinion was valid, the innovation team dismissed the challenge by saying, "The interviewees were unskilled." Can you guess what happened? The product adoption rate was near-zero. Another six months passed before the update addressed this basic requirement. As a result, the company lost untold millions in subscription business, simply because the team dismissed a challenge due to personal bias.

Before you reinvent the figurative wheel, you may find that some challenges can be addressed with activities such as marketing messaging, process change, cultural changes, or other shifts in internal or external behavior. These findings are critical. When creating the outputs from this step, determine whether you can initiate any activities immediately to benefit the organization. Teams often unearth pain points or customer needs that do not fit into the paradigm of the current project. Start to communicate those as soon as possible, because this information can be used to spin-off or create new teams.

When you come back from this step with overwhelming evidence that the theme which has been chosen is one that is not a rational challenge for your organization to pursue, you will need to bring closure to the project or pivot to an area of discovered need. This is not failure. Learning that is shared and used to make better decisions provides tremendous value.

Activity: Put Challenge into Action

Create the Challenge maps.

- ☐ Spin out areas that can be immediately addressed or should be pursued by additional projects.
- ☐ Ensure you have clear and comprehensive artifacts.

Stage 3: Enlighten

Introduction to the Enlighten Stage

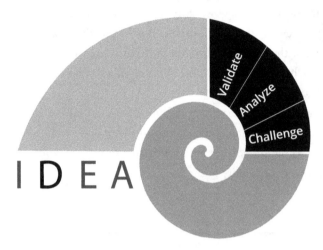

Figure 4.1 The Enlighten stage

In the Enlighten (E) stage, you reimagine a series of paths to solve the highest priority needs or eliminate challenges you have discovered. What makes this stage both challenging and beautiful is that it acknowledges that there is more than one way to solve a problem. You read that right. In most cases, there are, indeed, multiple ways to get from point A to point B (Figure 4.1).

In this stage, both you and the customer are enlightened. You understand the facts, the needs, and the challenges, then lead with a North Star mindset. You connect your vision to current customer conditions through a phased approach. This approach consists of three paths representing degrees of sophistication and completeness in solving the customers' problems balanced against the priorities, resources, and timelines of your organization.

Using your understanding of the challenges that need to be solved and your state-of-the-art learning from the Include stage, you can now

define the idealized behaviors or experiences that need to occur for your innovation to be successful. You then find solutions grounded in the reality of what you could deliver in the desired time frame. To test your idealized behavior, you craft stories about how the customer's world is better because you solved their problems in the ways you have defined. Then you give your customers the opportunity to edit the story. If you have not quite gotten the problem and/or the solution right, you rework the solutions and stories and share them again. You will start with a rough cut, refine, test, and then reiterate and refine until you have created a vision that aligns to your team's goals and priorities.

By spending the time doing informed problem solving and storytelling, you can understand and take into consideration the reaction of your audience to the proposal at a very low cost to your organization, while increasing the probability of success.

Enlighten Checklist

- ☐ Solve the challenges.
    - ☐ Create Run, Crawl, and Walk paths.
        - ☐ Conduct research spikes.
        - ☐ Create the journey and requirements document outputs.
    - ☐ Protect value (patents and so on).
    - ☐ Assess the ethical implications of your paths.
- ☐ Storytell.
    - ☐ Draw the storyboards.
    - ☐ Script the storyboards.
- ☐ Test the story.
    - ☐ Recruit interviews.
    - ☐ Run the feedback interviews.
    - ☐ Analyze the results.

Example: How Innovation: Africa's Implemented the Enlighten Stage

A great deal happens in this stage of our Innovation: Africa case study. As you visualize the data about the problems and the relationship between causes and effects, the solution(s) and priorities begin to reveal themselves. You realize in a leap of understanding that most of the problems stem from the lack of plentiful clean water, so you begin generating many questions and ideas about how to solve this problem.

Why not just pump water from a more developed area? Can you purify the surface water? Can you access groundwater? How would villagers access the water if a local source were created?

One by one, you evaluate and accept or reject the options. You cannot source water from elsewhere because the government and the people have no money to develop distribution mechanisms. Purifying the surface water is unsustainable because rain—the chief source of surface water—is unreliable due to extended droughts. But you know from geological maps that vast natural reservoirs of water rest below ground, if only you could tap them. What would that take? Obviously, a well. So why not just dig a well by hand and lift the water out with buckets, as has been done elsewhere for thousands of years? The answer: because in many areas, the groundwater is so deep that a pump would be required to bring it to the surface. Is there anyone available to drill a well without electric power? Yes. You identify someone who can bring in a rig powered by diesel, only to realize that there's no affordable or available, sustainable means of operating the electric pump.

The pre-existing problem or condition is that energy must be made available to run the pump to bring water up from below. You realize that solar energy is an inexpensive and sustainable solution because the sun is free and in unlimited supply year round. But your innovation cannot stop there. How will you distribute water from the pump to the people? How will the people afford to repair or replace the pump? You must have a plan for supporting the full lifecycle of the innovation. As you arrive at your innovation, you create storyboards to illustrate how the locals' world will be and engage them in affirming or pointing out gaps in your thinking. One challenge at a time, you create visions that illustrate how

the problems of water, power, medical care, nutrition, education, and income can be solved.

Solve the Challenges

As you enter this step, you have a detailed list of the challenges that align to your theme. You know which personas would benefit from your solutions. Your next job is to stand in the shoes of your future customers for a moment and imagine the experience that would solve the problems you have discovered and validated. You start to solve the challenges by creating a map of behaviors and experiences that describe idealized end states against which you will measure success. You then determine ways to meet the idealized behaviors and experiences that align with the resources, timeline, and feasibility of implementation that is rational for your organization.

The output of this step is one journey map for each idealized path you define. You may also have a text version of the requirement descriptions of each solution in its entirety. In some cases, the journey maps can be the same, but the actions taken to complete the steps may be different. Perhaps some steps are done manually in a short-term path, and automated or eliminated as you attain your long-term goals. This is because the challenges that you are solving are the same for the journey, but your ability to address the challenges may increase in complexity and sophistication as you advance.

At this step, you should expand your team with experts who have skills that can help you solve the challenges you identified. If you anticipate handing the innovation off to a secondary team for implementation, you would be wise to include members of that team in this discussion. This inclusion helps create organizational buy-in and guide the depth of the discussion before you present the information for activation approval.

Start Enlighten stage discussions by sharing your Discover stage relationship maps and journey maps. In each, highlight the challenges the team identified. Make sure everyone understands the issues. Discuss again which were the most critical, which were prioritized by the interviewees, and how many times they were raised. What are the preceding issues that may cause the challenge? What are the outcome impacts? As a team, discuss the challenges in depth before designing any solutions. If you find challenges that lack information your team needs to fully understand the root cause, go back and conduct more dedicated research to answer these questions. When you review the journeys in the extended team, you may increase understanding because you have added expertise and knowledge to the group to innovate and resolve the challenges.

Consider why the Compassion-Driven Innovation methodology does not ask you to jump right into solving the problem. You spent time in the Include stage creating a proto-journey map that enables you to clearly communicate what you considered and discarded (your informed guess). You spent time in the Discover stage validating through researching your proto-journey map and documenting the true journey. Finally, you mapped the challenges into that journey. Now your whole team can draw a direct correlation between the ideas you initially considered, the challenges you discovered, and the innovation you need to uncover.

As your team solves challenges, we recommend that you keep a journey map as a living document and update the maps after each discussion to reflect any new insights.

To provide an example of how to solve a challenge and update the journey, we can go back to the Innovation: Africa "Challenge" section. They discovered a condition that they realized they should have solved before or alongside providing electricity to the school. Even with the addition of light in the classroom, many children still did not attend school. This was because they were unwell and/or lethargic, not because of a lack of light. The Innovation: Africa team determined that the root cause of this problem was that the children were sick from drinking dirty surface water and suffered from malnutrition due to drought conditions. These pre-existing conditions had to be solved before other problems.

To prevent this type of oversight in the future, Innovation: Africa created a checklist with guiding insights (Figure 4.2).

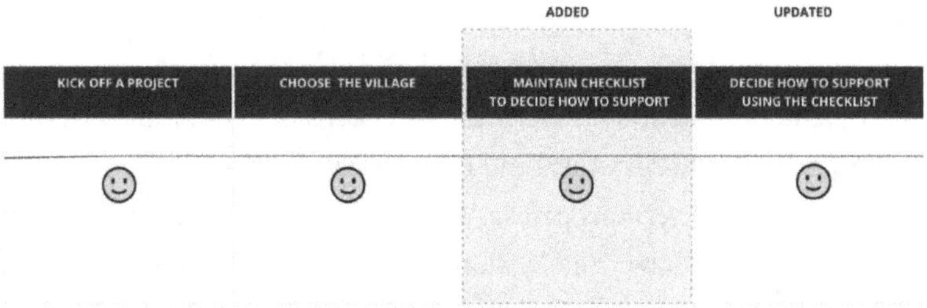

Figure 4.2 Example for Innovation: Africa after resolution of the challenges

In future projects, they listed all the ways the village they were evaluating needed support and ranked them by priority from high to low using the guiding checklist. After each project, they updated the checklist with any new insights.

If we look at this journey and create the "Challenge" map, we can see that the journey from their first project has a challenge noted in "decide how to support" before the first project.

Teams thrive in this step when members are willing to debate and offer alternate views. That is not always going to be the case. We have all been part of cultures in which team members tend to nod and agree too soon. This false agreement can result in catastrophe if you move forward to solve challenges while not actually agreeing on what the challenges mean. This often results in failure when innovation ideas are being implemented. While we cannot say definitively why this happens, from personal experience, we see a combination of vague language (one word or acronym represents multiple ideas), our desire to be agreeable, our discomfort with the team (and feeling insecure about expressing opinions), and our ego's wish to appear smart. When we use vague words or concepts to describe what we mean to build and everyone nods, we may all be thinking about completely different things.

Take time to assess if you believe your organization can have healthy debate. A culture where questions are welcomed and met without shame is a culture in which innovation can thrive.

Create Run, Crawl, and Walk Paths

Extensive writing has been done on the power of three and how it pervades our lives. Storytellers from orators to writers to advertisers use the "rule of three" to frame communications. In Latin, *omne trium perfectum* translates roughly to, "Every set of three is complete." The Compassion-Driven Innovation methodology builds on the power of three by recommending that you envision three versions of innovation that you can communicate to customers and internal stakeholders. Many planning practices call these versions paths. And we recommend creating them in the order of Run, Crawl, and Walk paths. These paths represent levels of effort and innovation required to implement a solution or set of solutions. You will not be choosing *between* the paths; you use the three paths to help your organization find their way forward.

- **Run** is the ideal solution, which often requires significant effort or using emerging or unproven technologies to achieve the goal. The Run path is the North Star vision in action.
- **Crawl** refers to the path that takes the least effort to solve some or all of the challenges identified.
- **Walk** is a longer-term effort than Crawl; it solves a larger set of challenges or solves them more elegantly with more forward-looking techniques.

You can choose to create your paths at any of the three levels or to build them in parallel. There is no right answer. However, our experience leads us to believe that starting with Run and then rationalizing efforts to come up with the Crawl and then Walk paths tends to produce more creative, customer-delighting results. Teams who are only tasked with long-term vision may choose to only create Run and Walk paths. Teams tasked with short-term vision are encouraged to create a Run path, but to set the time frame, feasibility, and effort to match their directive.

Here is why you need to create all three versions: The Run path storyboard should have the greatest value to the consumer. Showing the Run story to the interviewee will confirm the North Star vision. However, you will not be delivering the Run path right away. You need to determine whether the Crawl path adds enough value to the interviewee. Would someone adopt or spend money on your innovation in this path? You need to ensure that whatever you do in the short term will give you enough business to sustain the project so you can deliver your Run version later. The same concept applies to the Walk path. If you fail to increase the value in the Walk path over the Crawl path, you run the risk of the project being cancelled before you can get to the ultimate leg of the innovation journey, the Run path.

There are many ways to brainstorm and determine what is in each of the three paths. The Compassion-Driven Innovation methodology pares down best practices from multiple disciplines. In this section, we outline the minimum viable exercises we use to come up with the paths.

It makes things easier if you consider three things for each path:

- **Time frame:** This is the expectation your company has for when each path would be implemented.
- **Feasibility:** This is the likelihood that something could be accomplished. How much tolerance does your company have for risk in what you recommend from a technology perspective? Consider three categories:
  - **Likely:** The technology or concepts exist and are well enough understood that you could build what would need to be built using tools, materials, technologies, or processes that exist today.
  - **Probable:** The capabilities that exist today could be built on in a thoughtful manner to create what is needed.
  - **Possible:** The ideas are a leap beyond capabilities that exist today. The unknowns exceed the knowns in terms of ability to execute.
- **Effort:** This is a relative assessment of the resources required to achieve the desired timeline. Given your project's time frame and your organization's size, determine whether your paths should include efforts that are:
  - **Rational:** easily achievable
  - **Questionable:** possibly achievable
  - **Stretch:** unlikely to be achievable with the current resources.

For example:

- If your project is aimed at disruptive innovation that aims to shift fundamental aspects of how we live, you can aim for a Run path that looks out several years, where the feasibility is "Possible," and the effort is "Stretch."

- If your innovation needs to deliver short-term benefits to your organization, you should aim for a Crawl path that is just a few months long. This path should prioritize ideas and theories that are "Likely" to be achievable and "Rational" given your resources and required time frame.
- If your project targets longer-term innovation and you have the luxury of assembling more resources, you can aim for solutions that have a Walk path time frame of a year or so, where the feasibility is "Probable" or "Possible," and the effort is "Rational" or "Questionable."

Having this understanding ahead of time will aid in prioritizing the work and solutions you come up with for any path.

At a minimum, for each path you create, include a text-based description and a journey map. Using just text—typically in the form of a requirements document—to communicate the paths is inadequate to represent workflows and often results in a lack of clarity for your stakeholders. Using only maps results in representations that are too vague or high-level, leaving stakeholders to fill in too many details, which may result in misaligned expectations and disappointment as the project is activated. You *should not* create user interface designs or other high-fidelity views of a product or solution in this step. That will come later.

In each path, you will conduct research spikes and create multiple types of outputs. Research spikes are simulated exercises in which you try to prove or disprove ideas. Not every challenge that we solve needs to have a research spike. You should pursue one only if you have doubts about the solution. Some businesses call research spikes "stories," "projects," or "experiments."

How to Conduct Compassion-Driven Innovation Research Spikes

Research spikes are simulated exercises in which you try to prove or disprove ideas. The challenges you need to solve within any path may be complex, or you may realize when you try to solve it that you do not know enough and you need to deepen your research in that spike. If you cannot avoid the challenge and you are unsure how to solve it, start creating research spikes.

To craft an effective research spike, we frame a challenge in a manageable size and give it a title. Then, we define what one desired experience is. This is our hypothesis. We then define how we know we have succeeded, referred to as the *Done criteria*. Finally, we limit the scope of the work. (You may note that this reflects agile story techniques that go back decades.) This approach enables skilled people to be innovative with extreme focus. We trust the people assigned to a research spike to think through how to resolve the challenge.

When written in its entirety, each research spike will look something like this:

- **Title:**
- **Hypothesis:**
- **Done criteria:**
- **Scope:**

What this looks like in practice is simple. We illustrate this using a challenge from Innovation: Africa. Start by listing a challenge.

Innovation: Africa is facing a scaling challenge. They have successfully helped many villages in Uganda. However, their current office has reached their limits of support based on location and the numbers of supported villages. The challenge they face is: "To bring water to new villages in Uganda, we need to open a new regional office. We do not know whether we will have enough villages to warrant doing so."

Within this larger challenge, we could list a few smaller challenges:

- Funding a new central office must be completed up front. Sustaining a central office is currently only economically feasible if it is supporting at least 20 villages.
- Setting up a central office requires a water engineer, an electrical engineer and geologist, a civil engineer, and a field officer and manager.
- There are not 20 high-priority villages which are fully funded to support a new central office in the new area.

Next, you will determine which of these smaller challenges to prioritize first. If you have more than one group that can conduct research spikes, it is appropriate and expeditious to scope and perform multiple research spikes at once.

In this example, if you were to select the first challenge, your research spike title would be: "Funding a new central office must be completed up front. Sustaining a central office is currently only economically feasible if it is supporting at least 20 villages. Now state what the desired experience is. This will be the ideal outcome. For this example, you could state, "Expansion into a new region would be economically viable and sustainable because we have 20 fully funded villages. We also see the potential for additional villages in the area for future support." This is your hypothesis.

Now you must define how you will know you have succeeded in solving this issue. For our example, we will know we succeeded if we are able to enter into a new region with committed funding for 20 villages and a pipeline for the future. You could push this further and list specific artifacts or outputs from the step. Maybe you need the checklist guiding document that helps to decide which villages to support with the best ways to support them. Maybe you have a meeting with the village leaders where they agree to the partnership. The list of success metrics and outputs must be tangible and measurable.

Finally, limit the scope of the work. For each research spike, list the set of activities that you may try to achieve the goal. Innovation: Africa could craft a research spike to try training local residents to do self-assessment. They could look for other nonprofit teams or residents who are already in the area to help research. What is great about the use of research spikes is that you can figure out if the approach will fail before investing heavily in the idea. In this case, we know that this approach would not work, and that the team really needed direct resources in the local area. Research spike activities are only limited by your imagination. Refer back to the state-of-the-art research to see if you can build on other ideas.

You should limit research spikes in scope and time. If you have a particularly challenging issue, you can time-box the research spike by stating that you will spend no more than "x" days on the investigation. The team would report back at that time and discuss reshaping the research. You also could choose to failure-scope the investigation by stating that you will determine the research spike failed if a set of criteria is determined to be unachievable.

Put together, your research spike looks like this:

- **Title:** Funding a new central office must be completed up front.
- **Hypothesis:** Expansion into a new region would be economically viable and sustainable when we have 20 fully funded villages and we also see the potential for additional villages in the area for future support.
- **Done criteria:** We know this is done when we have:
  - A checklist guiding document that helps to decide which villages are reasonable to support
  - A determination regarding the highest-priority way to support each village
  - A way for village leaders to approve and commit to partnership.
- **Scope:** We will limit this research spike to 40 hours of effort for each team member.

An alternative or additive scope may be: The research team will investigate satellite communication tools, water depth assessment methods, and both paper and electronic means of performing the surveys. The results of the research spike will be the inputs to the journeys as you go through the Run, Crawl, and Walk exercises below.

You could track research spikes in any tool you prefer. Some teams use simple sticky notes on a physical or virtual board. Others work in online tools such as Smartsheet. Some prefer their company project tracking system. If you are from a technology company, you may already have some "backlog tools" at your disposal. These are simple online tools that let you create tasks and assign them to people working on your project. A quick search on "Free Online Scrum Tools" will help you find a tool if you do not like any of your existing options.

Basic Problem-Solving

There are as many ways to solve problems as there seem to be movies about illegal street racing—a near infinite number. Some approaches are more appropriate for certain types of problems than others. For example, if you are building a product, you may choose to use a simple clarification and breakdown method as taught by many quality product design consortiums. They typically include four steps:

1. **Break down the problem** into the smallest pieces: You completed this when you defined your research spikes.
2. **Generate ideas:** You may have completed this when you generated your hypothesis.
3. **Assess your ideas and rank them:** This is the output of the research spike.
4. **Implement the solutions**: We will get to that in the Activate stage. You do not want to build or implement something without evaluating how it fits into the larger picture.

If you are working on challenges that do not fit into the bounds of product problem-solving, consider using a version of behavioral science problem-solving. If this is something that interests you, a myriad of exceptional books on behavioral science exist. We suggest looking for ones that address your specific market and target customer. In a simplification of the process of problem-solving using behavioral science approaches, you:

1. **List the challenges.** You already completed this when you defined the research spike.
2. **Identify behaviors you want to add or change.** This will make your research spike definition more specific and may lead into a hypothesis definition.
3. **Identify different ways you could change that behavior** by adding or removing triggers or specific activities. You may do this as part of your hypothesis/scoping, or it may be an output of the research spike.
4. **Measure the changes against the goals of the personas** you have identified. Did you solve the challenges in a way that was aligned to the persona's goals and your organizational goals?

Note that behavioral science problem-solving does not include implementing the changes; it covers objective assessment and measurement

of changes that directly or indirectly cause changes in behaviors. This method, as you may infer from the name, is best suited for issues related to human behavior.

Create the Run Path: The North Star

To reimagine the future that is your Run vision, unleash your mind from the constraints of how things have been done to date. When setting a North Star, you want to think as far ahead as your organization can imagine. In some cases, where the organization is focused on short-term gains, this could be a one-year vision. In other cases, where you are part of an organization taking a longer perspective, you may want to think 5 to 10 years ahead. In either case, you must align with strategic initiatives and goals if you want your vision to be accepted and activated.

Describe in text and in a journey map a version of the journey that solves every challenge you uncovered in the Discover stage.

Most people read that sentence and get stuck. This is where persistence and invention are your friends. If you cannot envision a version of the journey, you need to craft some research spikes as we describe previously.

Consider your most important persona. Describe a journey for that persona that avoids *many* of the challenges on your map. Choose a remaining challenge and craft a research spike for it: List the state that happens right before you hit the challenge. List what the output has to be. Talk to people in your expanded consulting circle for ideas on what you might want to try. Then use the research spikes process to try different ways to address or avoid the challenge.

In the Run path, you can consider expanding state-of-the-art and putting together new technologies that would help alleviate the challenge in some small way. When you have an idea that may work, add that to the journey. Select the next open challenge and approach it the same way. Continue to iterate on all challenges that remain open. When you have one persona with a successful story, move on to the next one and repeat the process.

Remember that, during this process, you want to solve the persona challenges *and* rethink the way the journey works. Eliminate steps.

Eliminate personas. Bring in new personas that add strength and value in the journey. Draw that. Describe it in text.

Once you have your important personas covered, take into consideration those who would be opposed to you solving the challenges. Craft research spikes to discover ways to add value to the paths.

Science fiction writers and product managers do these exercises in their sleep. But for the rest of us, creating a narrative may not be so intuitive. When in doubt, make Mad Libs.[1] Outline a story in sentences, leaving blanks for the unknowns. Using any buyer map, lifecycle, or journey map you just created, replace each step with a description of what the experience would be like if you eliminated all challenges. If this sounds too much like magic, the following examples would be helpful.

Example of the Run Path for Innovation: Africa

Figure 4.3 illustrates the Innovation: Africa Run path.

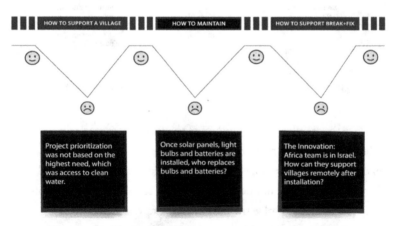

Figure 4.3 Example of Innovation: Africa before Crawl, Walk, and Run paths

Along their journey, Innovation: Africa had to overcome several challenges to reach the Run state. Their approach was based on small incremental improvements in which they learn from one project to another

---

[1] "MadLibs." https://madlibs.com/

how to improve their operations. To simplify an example, we can assume that Innovation: Africa's journey map (Figure 4.3) contains three groups of challenges:

- The project was not based on the highest need, which is access to clean water.
- Once the solar panels, lights, and batteries were installed, the villagers could not afford to replace the bulbs or batteries.
- The Innovation: Africa team is located in Israel. The team needs a way to handle break and fix situations, especially after the installation is complete and the team members return to Israel.

Figure 4.4 Example of the Run path for Innovation: Africa

Once they resolve all these groups of challenges, they reach the outcome of the Run state (Figure 4.4). Many project teams cannot resolve all challenges in one day for various reasons, such as time constraints, limited budget, technology that is not developed yet, and so on. The way to approach these constraints is to solve the problems in Crawl and Walk paths.

Example of the Run Path for Gutter Tex

In the Gutter Tex journey map, Daniel found three main challenges (Figure 4.5):

- The quote process introduced friction through on-premises meetings that require homeowner presence.

- The scheduling process required multiple communication steps.
- The installation process was manually coordinated and optimized.

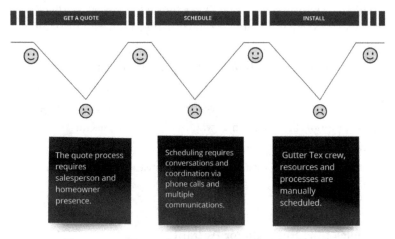

Figure 4.5 Example of Gutter Tex before Crawl, Walk, and Run paths

Daniel's compassion for both the customer and the employees was key to figuring out how to truly innovate. He shifted Gutter Tex to resolve each of these challenges in their Run path in a way that could create delight for customers and employees alike.

We can envision their Run state like this (Figure 4.6):

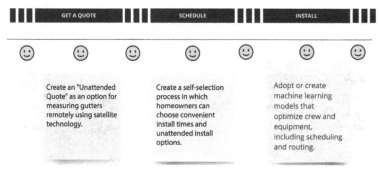

Figure 4.6 Example of the Run path for Gutter Tex

You will note that he has solved each of the major challenges, building on learning from prior steps. He met his desire to meet the needs of his customers, sales team, and his installation crew. His use of automated measurement options for the quote process dramatically simplifies the salesperson's job. The online process for homeowners to choose their comfort level with salesperson interaction aligns personal preferences with actual experiences, and scheduling automation optimizes installation crew productivity.

Where Daniel shines is not explicitly called out on this path, but it needs to be recognized. This type of a vision is only possible because Daniel has built up a business with massive numbers of five-star ratings. The core assumption that a customer would be able to trust Gutter Tex without meeting the owner and teams up front relies on the long and deep history he has of building a business which treasures their customers and employees alike.

Example of the Run Path for AceraEI

The Run path for AceraEI envisions transforming public school systems. They see the tools as part of their nationally available education platform (Figure 4.7).

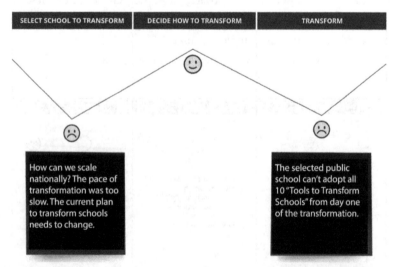

Figure 4.7 Example of AceraEI before Crawl, Walk, and Run paths

They see achieving this through creation, funding, and rollout of the full 10 "Tools to Transform Schools." Each school opts-in one tool at a time (Figure 4.8).

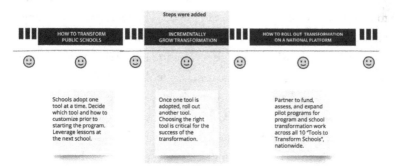

Figure 4.8 Example of the Run path for AceraEI

Run Path Summary

The Run path illustrates the optimism and type of vision you must harness to reach higher levels of innovation. People often ask us when we know we have a Run path that is "good." The answer for many is either feeling excited or a sense of lightness at thinking about a solution that seems entirely preposterous but needs to exist.

Once you have a vision that is sufficiently optimistic, solves all the challenges, and pushes the boundaries of rational thinking (as directly aligned to your theme), take the time to create a journey map, a relationship map, and detailed description documents.

Create the Crawl Path: Where Vision Meets Reality

The Crawl path is where vision meets cold, hard reality. You will create a Crawl path when you need to connect your innovation to a business unit or when you need to show how to add value in incremental steps. Determine what timeline would be acceptable to your organization. Do you need to show a plan that takes two months of effort, one year, or two years of effort? This has to be considered before you can effectively define your Crawl path. In larger organizations, one-year plans are a rational crawl path. In smaller organizations, such as Gutter Tex, the Crawl path could be closer to a sixty- or ninety-day plan.

Look at your Challenge map and then look at your Run path vision. You must create a Crawl definition that at a minimum adds enough value to your customers that they can justify adoption. You also want to attempt to add incremental innovation from the Run path that is rational to complete and bring to market in the Crawl time frame. Advancing or combining state-of-the-art is an important technique for innovation in a Crawl path. Revisit the Include stage artifacts. Iterating on, combining, or repurposing existing processes or tools can often create massive improvements in experience with relatively low effort.

Run research spikes to look for effective ways to solve challenges in your given effort and time frame. Capture each of the improvements in a Crawl path journey map. You must add enough value to the personas by solving challenges that are of high value to ensure that the solution would be viable in the market. It is normal for this set of improvements to feel iterative and not yet innovative.

Document what this Crawl path could look like. Identify and further investigate which state-of-the-art techniques would be used. Where there are holes in your solution, you will need to conduct research spikes to resolve them.

While you are imagining the short-term path, identify new marketing messaging, sales techniques, and minor improvements that can boost your customer experience and productivity in the near term. Share these findings with your organization as soon as possible. Check your Crawl path against the Challenge map to verify that you are solving high-priority challenges. Defining short effort paths that do not add value will result in low adoption and possible cancellation of the larger vision.

Example of the Crawl Path for Innovation: Africa

The Crawl path for Innovation: Africa became clear after examining the results of the first project in 2008. The organization installed two solar panels in a village in Tanzania to provide electricity to their medical center, only to discover that access to clean water was a bigger issue. As a result, Sivan created a new process to fully understand the highest need that will also provide return on investment (ROI) for each village. By using the highest need checklist, the Innovation: Africa team can determine which need to address in which order (Figure 4.9).

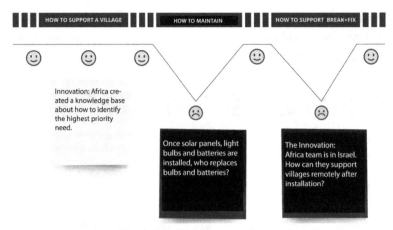

Figure 4.9 Example of Innovation: Africa Crawl path

Example of the Crawl Path for Gutter Tex

In the Gutter Tex Crawl path, we know that the team resolved the first challenge by adding the option for an unattended quote and inspection. This option enabled them to remove the first point of friction and increase homeowner satisfaction and the likelihood of homeowners accepting quotes. With their many positive online reviews and referenceable customers, they were able to establish enough trust to make this a viable option (Figure 4.10).

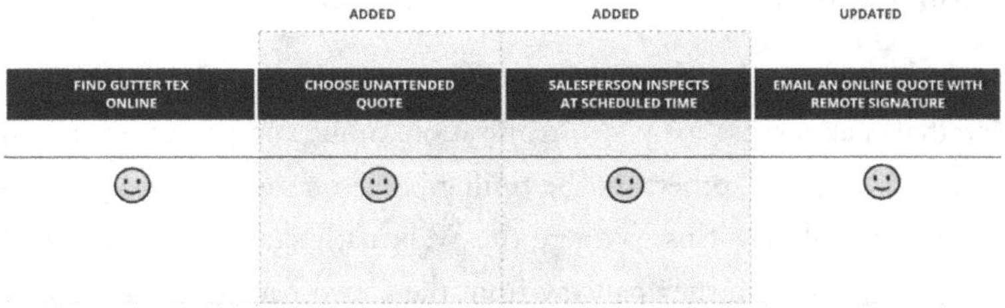

Figure 4.10 Example of Gutter Tex Crawl path

Example of the Crawl Path for AceraEI

AceraEI stepped back and sliced their Run path work into a short-term plan. They determined that they could help the public schools in their

district and the area around Acera School to transform by starting with one tool. They would then learn from the public school rollout experience and use their findings in the next path (Figure 4.11).

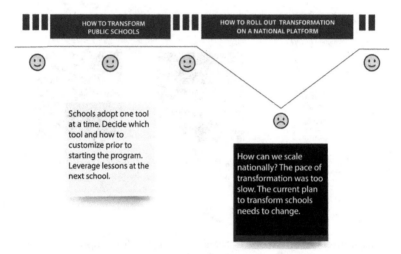

Figure 4.11 Example of AceraEI Crawl path

Crawl Path Summary

The point of the Crawl path is to pick only the lowest fruit and achieve fast time-to-value in a way that aligns to your theme and timelines.

Create the Walk Path: A Midrange Approach

Find a point between your Crawl path timeline and your Run path time-line that makes sense for your organization. Some companies set this to be a midway point, others set the timing based on their company prior-ities or capabilities. This is where the Walk path should land. Imagine how to bring the journey halfway from the Crawl path to the Run path using your timeline and resources. Redraw the journeys to represent the mid-term efforts. Again, conduct research spikes. Consider and consult with others about how to implement the Walk path. Identify and fur-ther investigate which state-of-the-art techniques would be used. Iden-tify story and implementation gaps for further investigation and present opportunities for innovation.

Look for versions of the journey which leapfrog entire steps in the process, combining or avoiding the customer's challenges altogether. This path should aim to solve many of the biggest challenges in the Challenge map. The output of this path will be one or more journey maps and text descriptions of the requirements to achieve the path.

Example of the Walk Path for Innovation: Africa

Figure 4.12 depicts the Innovation: Africa Walk path.

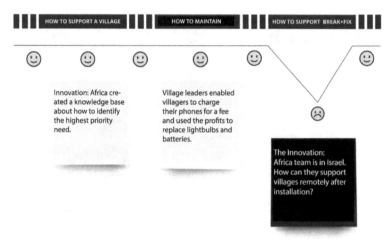

Figure 4.12 Example of Innovation: Africa Walk path

In the Walk path, the Innovation: Africa team is resolving the challenges somewhere between what they accomplished in the Crawl path and what is left to resolve to achieve the Run path. After they establish a consistent way to invest in the highest need of the selected village, the next question is, "What are the critical challenges we need to tackle so the village becomes self-sustaining?" From the first solar panel installations, they had four years until light bulbs and batteries would need to be replaced. During this time, they had to conceive a solution for how the village could generate income to pay for the light bulbs and batteries, and how the villagers would be trained to do so. A breakthrough discovery was that—even though the locals live in some of the poorest conditions imaginable and without electricity—many of them owned cell phones that must be charged. Locals gathered phones and

traveled on foot for many hours to pay pennies to charge the phones in a village that had electricity. Within a few days of offering the same service while eliminating the need to travel, the village was generating an income that could pay for maintenance of the solar panel batteries and light bulbs.

Example of the Walk Path for Gutter Tex

Figure 4.13 shows the Gutter Tex Run path.

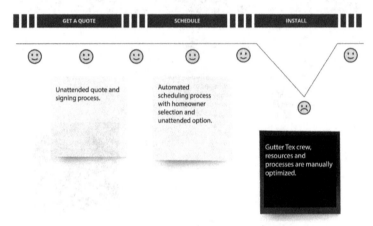

Figure 4.13 Example of Gutter Tex Walk path

Daniel used the Walk path to take on the second largest point of friction for his customers—the scheduling process and at-home installation requirement. The Gutter Tex team created an online agreement option that enabled them to perform contactless, unattended installations for customers who preferred a "no hassles" approach. This innovation in the process eliminated the two largest homeowner challenges.

However, because the Walk path would take longer than Daniel wanted to wait to innovate, the team reconsidered the ways that they could optimize the "get a quote" process. A technology-minded business owner, Daniel envisioned using satellite maps and online imagery that were readily available to help generate initial home measurements and calculations. Equipped with the extended detail, salesperson onsite visits and inspections were also reduced in scope and time.

Example of the Walk Path for AceraEI

In the Walk path, AceraEI helps public schools adopt additional tools incrementally. They gather data about the transformation and conduct research on how to enhance the 10 "Tools to Transform Schools" so the toolkit can be more readily adopted nationwide. The research will be funded by companies that partner with AceraEI. The result of this path is that the 10 "Tools to Transform Schools" will be ready for national rollout (Figure 4.14).

Walk Path Summary

In scoping your walk path, consider innovation you can accomplish part way between the Crawl and Run paths. What novel solution aspects can you bring to the challenges? Also note that there is value in continuing to innovate on the challenges you solved in the Walk path.

Once you have defined your paths, it is time to prepare to evangelize or share the solutions that you have created. Before you do, you should consider how you need to protect the value you have created.

Protect Generated Value

You may have created intellectual property when conducting your research. Ensure that your organization protects the value of what you have created to date. For example, consider whether you want to generate internal or external papers on what you have learned. You may consider other formal or informal methods of protecting the ideas which you have generated in the path creation.

Assess the Ethical Implications

Why does ethics matter for innovators? Because the future is born out of our imaginations. As innovators, we must be conscious about the decisions we make. We must put ourselves in the shoes of the people who will use or be impacted by our technology. Do you feel confident that what you are creating is doing no harm?

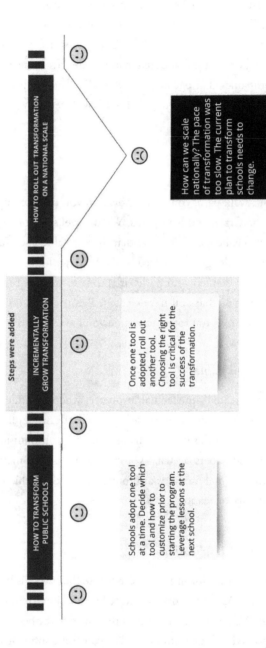

Figure 4.14 Example of AceraEI after Walk path

As innovators, we are attempting to solve challenges in new ways by optimizing journeys, eliminating steps, and inventing new processes, services, or products. Along the way, we must be conscious of whether what we are innovating is ethical—typically defined as well understood standards of right and wrong. For the purpose of this book, we only address a small portion of a large topic and hope you further explore using the resources available from institutions such as the Markkula Center for Applied Ethics or the Harvard Center for Ethics.

Companies have been accused of deceptively causing user behavior by triggering or automating actions without the express consent of users and of using their data in ways that are not transparent. Various reports suggest that some social media sites use these methods to cause addictive behavior patterns. We can use this example as an opportunity to learn from the perceived mistakes of others. When solutions are created without the end users' explicit understanding and consent to what was happening, we have what many would consider an ethical breach.

What should you do to avoid this problem? Spend time brainstorming the implications of your innovations. Determine the ways in which they could impact humanity and the planet. Think through both the positive and negative consequences of what you are proposing. Are there safeguards that need to be put in place to ensure that the solution is ethical, humane, and aligned with your organization's (and your personal) values?

Another way to think about ethics is to think about trustworthiness. Has your company established a practice of delivering trustworthy solutions? Trustworthiness means different things in different industries, but it is typically enabled by transparency. Transparency can be measured by whether your users understand what is happening and make informed decisions.

If your solution incorporates artificial intelligence (AI), you must think far beyond simple transparency or the ability to explain how the AI model was trained and makes decisions. You must ensure that what you are creating is not accidentally introducing bias or rights violations in areas such as surveillance and privacy. IEEE has established "Ethics in

Action"[2] resources that include papers and practical advice on how differ-ent industries and areas should take a pragmatic approach to this topic. In addition, the World Economic Forum provides a "12-step guide" for practicing AI ethics.[3] Many industry-specific and technology-specific eth-ics committee resources are also available for you to explore.

Considering and ensuring ethical innovation is the responsibility of everyone who participates in a project. Have the hard ethics conversations among your team before you begin to evangelize solutions to other larger organizations.

Activity: Put Solve into Action

☐ Define your timelines and priorities.
☐ Create run, crawl, and walk paths.
☐ Conduct research spikes.
☐ Create the journey and requirements document outputs.
☐ Protect value (patents and so on).
☐ Assess the ethical implications of your paths.

Storytell

Before you spend a great deal of time building prototypes, you need unbi-ased proof that your Crawl, Walk, and Run paths are directionally correct and add value for customers. If you define a Crawl path that adds little value, you will fail to get adoption and you will never achieve your Walk innovation.

How can you present each version of the journey to your potential customers and get feedback on whether it resonates? We propose a very

---

[2] IEE.org. 2021. "IEEE Ethics in Action in Autonomous and Intelligent Systems." ethicsinaction.ieee.org (accessed April 24, 2021).
[3] World Economic Forum. September 11, 2020. "How to Put AI Ethics into Practice: A 12-Step Guide." www.weforum.org/agenda/2020/09/how-to-put-ai-ethics-into-practice-in-12-steps/

old-fashioned approach ripped from cartooning—storyboarding. Storyboarding is a visual way to describe the major events in a journey that is easy for others to follow. Think about a comic strip. The author tells the story in just a few frames. You know the main plot points with minimal frames and text.

Craft a low-resolution, low-fidelity visual translation of the story that describes your paths. You will note within the storyboards where improvements can be made to target the customer's existing experience. You are not designing a product; your goal is to convey the three paths in a way that can be easily understood by the customers to gain validation and by your peers to get organizational buy-in.

You can put together storyboards using whatever tool you are most comfortable with. Slides are low-cost, highly accessible methods of creating the story visualization. Interactive design tools, such as Sketch and Adobe XD, enable fast, low-fidelity visualization. Interactive boards, such as Miro, Figma or Lucidspark, can use frames to build a story and enable quick note-taking for interaction and recording feedback. If you are a pencil-to-paper person with some drawing skills, you can upload the pages to share. Do what works for your team and your organization. You share this visual story so everyone understands what is being proposed and can give feedback so you can iterate using this low-cost method.

We recommend that you keep the visual simple. If you make the story look like a highly polished presentation or a fully thought out design, you risk losing out on genuine feedback. Many people feel uncomfortable criticizing completed products. A secondary issue could occur as you start to show the storyboards around your internal organization. You are working with a small team now and have not yet made your larger team feel invested in the solution. Presenting a polished set of paths may make others feel excluded and as if their feedback is not welcome or wanted. Stick with sketches and resist the temptation to perfect the visual design.

Script the Storyboards

Once you have the storyboard, write the script you will read or, if you prefer, make detailed notes to keep yourself on point as you walk through the

story. The script or detailed notes should match your proposed journey for the path you are showing. Much like in the Validate step, talk through the storyboard so you can analyze the feedback and ensure that you tell the same story to each interviewee.

Use this as an opportunity to partner with team members who are skilled in communication and the process of storytelling. Include phrases and questions to determine how the innovation should be discussed and communicated to each persona.

You need to get the customer to say, "Yes, that resonates," or "You missed this big step," or, "Not interesting," or (the best information you can get if you miss the mark): "That is wrong."

Example of the Storyboard and Script for Innovation: Africa

Following is an example of a storyboard for Innovation: Africa's first project. With this storyboard, the Innovation: Africa team can validate the proposed solution with villagers for feedback and acknowledge any objections before deciding on supporting this village.

While generally we suggest that you use low-fidelity drawings or images for the reasons described earlier, there may be a time in which using photos in your storyboard can be helpful, such as when working with a village in subsequent projects, so that you can show that the solutions are real and work for other villages (Figure 4.15).

Example the Storyboard and Script for Gutter Tex

The Gutter Tex storyboard (Figure 4.16) illustrates that mixed illustrations, icons, and photos can be effective in showing what has already happened along a path, and what the incremental steps to be developed are (illustrations and icons).

Example of the Storyboard and Script for AceraEI

In this example for AceraEI, illustrations are used to highlight the full story, not just the "Tools to Transform Schools." The introductory storyboard introduces the assertions and challenges. The middle frames include as much detail as plausible to describe the solution and facilitate

Villagers drink contaminated water and get sick. They need access to clean water.

Clean water is available deep underground so a pump is installed.

A water tower is built.

Solar panels are installed to produce energy to pump the underground water.

The installation is complete.

The villagers have access to clean water.

Figure 4.15 Storyboard with images for Innovation: Africa subsequent projects (Photos courtesy of Innovation: Africa)

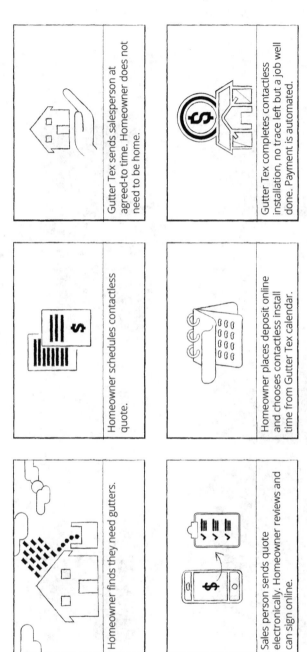

Figure 4.16 Example of a storyboard for Gutter Tex

Figure 4.17 Example of a storyboard for AceraEI

conversations with stakeholders. The storyboards close with the outcome statement (Figure 4.17).

As you can see from the previous examples, the depth and type of information in the storyboards will vary based on the project.

Activity: Put Storytell into Action

☐ Draw the storyboards.
☐ Script the storyboards.

Test the Story

Up until now, the Compassion-Driven Innovation methodology has highlighted the value of nonleading interviews. Now you need to flip that perspective. You are going to go on a roadshow to share your storyboards with your buyers and users from your relationship maps. Your job is not to sell the story; your job is to gauge whether the storyboard and script sell themselves.

You will bring all three versions of each story to unbiased contacts that represent the personas for which you want to innovate. You will get feedback on each of the versions of the innovation. You will make note of where your story missed the mark so you can update your storyboards. Ask yourself: "What are the missing components? What resonates, and what does not? You may feel like you are personifying the furniture and porridge in the Goldilocks children's story. You'd be right. In truth, you are exercising a Compassion-Driven Innovation version of the Goldilocks principle.[4]

Much like in the Discover stage, your goal is not to prove yourself correct. Your goal is to refine and build the three story paths which drive business and innovation that resonate with the personas.

---

[4] Wikipedia: The Free Encyclopedia. 2021. "Goldilocks Principle." https://en.wikipedia.org/wiki/Goldilocks_principle (accessed April 24, 2021).

Recruit

Decide exactly how many people you want to try your story out on for each persona. The number is completely up to you. We find that you must talk to six to eight people who represent a single persona or segment to start to see trends. If the project proposed will cost an exceptional amount of money, you will likely want to increase the number of people you interview so you can get a higher level of confidence in your results.

Track your research by creating a spreadsheet that includes a company name, the contact name (if you have it), persona they represent, email, last contact attempt, and the current status. Feel free to revisit people you interviewed in the past but remember not to fall into the trap of only interviewing people with whom you are very familiar or comfortable.

From here, you can either recruit interviewees by networking with your colleagues or hire an external agency to do so. Sourcing interviewees through colleagues has the advantage of representing your current customer and contact base effectively. You may be able to better predict which contacts are familiar with your areas of research.

On the other hand, sourcing interviews externally can help you achieve a less biased and wider variety of representation. Partnering with external interview agencies is also a great option if you need to create large outreach quickly or if you want to arrange for anonymous interviews through their services. You may do the interviews through a phone bridge they provide, or their researchers may conduct the interviews for you. The agency's team will not be emotionally attached to the storyboards and may be more comfortable identifying where interviewees are dissatisfied with a proposal. You will need to train the interviewees in depth in your story so that they are able to respond to requests for clarification or elaboration.

If you choose to go the internal route, start by sharing the spreadsheet and interview scripts with your colleagues and asking for help. Describe the personas in sufficient detail so that your colleagues can easily search for and make recommendations. Track their outreaches while recruiting interviewees on your own. Tracking enables you to ask for help from more people if recruiting or interviewing are delayed. If you are not keeping records, you will be hard pressed to define success and get help before you fail.

Consider Nondisclosure Agreements

You should consider putting nondisclosure agreements in place with interviewees. If your path storyboards contain strategic value or confidential or proprietary details, you will need to protect that as intellectual property your organization owns. If you are in doubt or need the form, check with your legal department or leadership team before you start conducting interviews.

Run the Feedback Interview

When you have your list of interviewers and any required nondisclosure agreements are executed, you or your external researchers should approach the interviews much like you did the nonleading interviews in the Discover stage. Use best practices in hosting. Script or make talking points for your storyboard; then perform, record, and listen to a few interviews to ensure that the script and storyboards are adequate to obtain the feedback you need. Once you are satisfied with the results, you can scale the number of interviews, continuing to record and make notes.

As you start your interview, explain that you are about to discuss an imagined vision. Be clear that the information you are showing is for validation purposes only and is not currently available for use. Request that your interviewee provide feedback and ask questions while you are discussing the storyboards. This will give you the opportunity to find where holes exist in your explanation or design.

Starting with the Run path, walk through each step or page using the notes or script you created. When you are in the middle of the story, pause and ask whether the interviewee has any questions or feedback. When you complete the Run path story, ask the interviewee what they liked about the story, while taking detailed exact notes. Then ask what was missing. Ask if there are any pain points that this does not solve for them. Ask if they have any ideas to improve the story. Then ask them an anchor question that lets you rank how much they "like" the proposal. We suggest a scale question such as, "Would you buy this solution if it were available?" with "Yes," "Maybe," and "No" responses. If a user is not willing to buy this solution, ask what is missing. What else would need to be part of the vision to justify their investment? If that is not sufficient, create a question with a scale that is meaningful to you. Your goal in the anchor question is to be able to filter feedback when analyzing the results. You can group people who were not interested together, those who were very interested together, and those who responded with "maybe" together to identify trends. Be sure to refine the Run path with this user before moving forward, as it may impact your Crawl and Walk paths.

Next, go to the Crawl storyboard and script. You will again use the script or talking points you created to walk them through the storyboard. Ask if the story solves enough challenges that they would consider adapting their current behavior to take advantage of the innovation. If you are investigating a paid service or product, you may want to ask how they would determine ROI for this new path. Understanding the ROI can give you a way to estimate exactly what someone may pay for your innovation and help you later determine in the Activate stage if it is a reasonable path to invest in or to help others determine how much to invest. Then ask them the same anchor question as in the Run path to rank how much they "like" the proposal.

Close the conversation by thanking them for their time and insights. If they had suggestions, you may request the ability to follow up for clarification in the future.

Analyze the Results

We find it most helpful to break down the feedback by path. Look at the path feedback as a collective by analyzing your anchor question results. Did the majority of the interviewees like the path? Which path had the highest ranking? It should be the Run path, but sometimes in pushing the envelope, you can push too far. Did you create enough perceived value in the Crawl path?

Use the interviewees' comments to create a quantified measurement of which steps resonate on each path.

Consider whether you need to reprioritize, pivot, or change your path content or solutions. You may need to go back to the Solve steps and run some new research spikes to solve newly discovered or missed challenges. You may also wish to find new ways of driving higher value using the interviewee's answer to how they would calculate the ROI.

If you get the story right on the first round, with no major missing pieces or assertions, go back to your challenge map. Did you inadvertently miss any of the pain points you previously identified? Can you make the storyboards even more enticing by solving one more problem? Can you take out any pieces and still achieve the same level of value?

Perform a cleanup and refinement of the storyboards, ask additional prospects or customers to validate them, and then get ready to start internal buy-in!

Activity: Put Test into Action

- ☐ Recruit interviews.
- ☐ Run the feedback interviews.
- ☐ Analyze the results.

Stage 4: Activate

Introduction to the Activate Stage

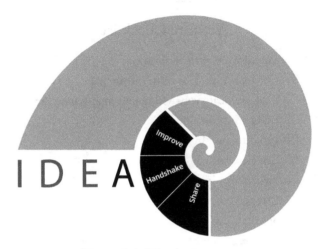

Figure 5.1 The Activate stage

How often have you heard colleagues say something like, "I came up with that idea years ago and no one implemented it?" If we had to wager a guess, it is because they did not complete the steps that we outline in the Activate stage (Figure 5.1).

Internal adoption of innovative ideas requires significant effort. Generally speaking, the amount of effort and the number of challenges are proportionate to the size of the organization and the extent to which decision making is distributed. Particularly in larger organizations, your small innovation team may not be the team that will determine which path will be funded nor the team that will implement the innovation. Regardless, if you do not work through the Activate stage, all of the amazing work you have done up to this point may only ever live "on paper" or in someone's memory.

In the Activate stage, your team considers and addresses the needs of the extended team who will approve and build on the innovation you have illuminated. You will identify organizational stakeholders and work to gain their support. You will partner to build prototypes and ensure

 Activate

project success with detailed artifacts for what the organization has approved. When you have completed the handoff, you will perform an assessment of how your project went and make changes in the process you will follow in your next project.

Activate Checklist

- ☐ Prepare to share your innovation.
  - ☐ Build your internal relationship map.
  - ☐ Communicate your vision and incorporate input.
  - ☐ Build your presentations.
  - ☐ Conduct buy-in meetings.
  - ☐ Ask for what you need.
- ☐ Formalize your innovation with a handshake.
  - ☐ Extend your team to add resources for prototyping.
  - ☐ Resolve or complete journey steps that can be completed.
  - ☐ Create high-fidelity prototypes.
  - ☐ Perform research spikes where needed to resolve missing pieces.
  - ☐ Complete the Crawl path or high-fidelity prototypes with expanded teams.
- ☐ Measure and improve your process.
  - ☐ Run a retrospective meeting with your team to review what went wrong and right in the process.
  - ☐ Add all findings to your existing checklists and processes.

Example of Imagine Innovation: Africa's Activate Stage

Back to our Innovation: Africa case study: In this stage, you work with your team to take the innovation from concept to reality, so that it can be executed as seamlessly as possible across the chosen villages. You will ensure a smooth transition by curating and transferring artifacts and understanding, while introducing stakeholders who will have an ongoing role in the implementation. Artifacts might include:

- An execution plan for the pilot project to solve the first problem in a selected village, followed by a rollout to the remaining villages in priority order. This may be repeated for each additional problem to be solved.
- A journey map that shows how each problem is resolved.
- A storyboard that illustrates how the locals in the village will live and how they will maintain the proposed innovation once it is available.
- Personas that describe the roles and skill sets necessary to complete the projects.
- Details about other resources needed across the lifecycle of the innovation.

Prepare to Share

Your goal is to leave this step with a plan to which all internal stakeholders agree. To achieve this, determine who is in your internal relationship map. Share your project findings with your highest priority influencers, buyers, and other impacted people. Next, iterate until you have a funded go-forward plan or have determined that you will deprioritize the project. You approach this step with the same discipline that you used in customer outreach and validation.

If this feels daunting, we get it. Communication strategy and political savvy are not everyone's strong suit. They do not have to be. But you do need team members who are experts dedicated to filling this important purpose. We have found in our professional travels through many organizations that individuals successful in product management, program management, sales, marketing, and corporate liaisons are often particularly skilled at understanding the right people to influence when and how, so that projects will move forward. If you haven't already recruited such a talent to your team, you should start networking.

Build Your Internal Relationship Map

Tapping the relationship mapping skills that you used in the Discover stage, you need to build an internal relationship map. List your internal buyers. These are the individuals who must endorse or approve your innovation for it to move forward. To the left, list the influencers—those who may impact the decisions but not necessarily make them. Now, most importantly, consider who would be impacted by your proposal. List the people and teams who might be the implementers of the innovation, or who might be called on to change their sales or marketing approaches, or otherwise might be involved in the execution of the chosen path. These are all influencers.

Next, instead of a Buyer column, create a Decision Maker column. These are the people you must make requests of and those who are gatekeepers to the final outcome. Include those with resourcing, strategic ownership, and funding approval powers.

Finally, list the specific requests that you must make to each decision maker. You need to be clear about what you need from each of the individuals. If there is a specific outcome, write it down. Know what to request at the end of each conversation to close the sale (Figure 5.2).

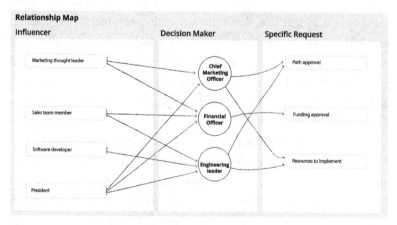

Figure 5.2 Depiction of a simplified relationship map to use in creating the activate plan

Failing to understand this entire relationship map is a major reason that innovation paths do not receive approval. If you do not sell the influencers on the idea—even if the direct consumers of the innovation like it—you may not get the funding you need. If you cannot convince those who will be impacted by bringing the innovation to life (such as the development, marketing, or sales teams), the innovation will perish before it gets out the door.

You will want to create personal relationships with as many people in your relationship map as possible by leveraging the diversity of your team to your advantage. If you have a trusted team member in sales, send that person to communicate to the sales stakeholders. Your goal is to build as many trusted bridges as possible so that the teams are genuinely invested in helping to make the innovation successful. You do not do this for your own personal benefit, but because this is the way to move the organization forward. Do not mistake generating good relationships and communicating with manipulation. Under no circumstances should you use personal or professional power or deception to increase the likelihood of adoption of an innovation.

Communicate Your Vision and Incorporate Input

Never underestimate the power of communication. When you communicate clearly, you can generate organizational buy-in and move your Crawl, Walk, and Run paths forward. Communicate poorly, and you may fail to see your path implemented. You can increase the probability of communicating well by knowing your audience, taking the time to align your message to their key values, and using communication styles that favor their communications preferences. For example, some people prefer presentations, while others prefer more casual conversations in a question and answer format.

Think through the interests and motivations of each of the people on your relationship map. They will not all be the same.

To simplify the number and types of communication, determine whether you can combine some of the people in your organizational relationship map together. Perhaps you can group them into similar profiles. For each group, consider the types of information they would need to understand whether your team's innovation paths are aligned with their organization's priorities and motives.

Build Your Presentation

If you are unsure how to start, there is a pretty standard way to collect the information in a way that spells out the story for the audience. In its simplest form, your outline will include:

- Purpose of the conversation (the request)
- Definition of the original project
- The state-of-the-art that is important to understand
- The challenges you discovered
- The reason the challenges must be solved
- The proposals
- The actions to take next
- Reiterate the request for this audience.

To pull this information together, revisit the artifacts you created in the first three stages (Include, Discover, and Enlighten). Make sure that you tailor the presentation toward the audience, including the level of detail that is relevant to the purpose of the meeting.

Determine for each internal stakeholder which techniques of communication are most meaningful for them. Consider both the environment and the format.

When considering your presentation, think through how much detail should go into any visualization of the paths. We have seen one too many conversations get wrapped around an axle because the team forgot the basic rules of matching the depth of fidelity (detail) to the audience. You may think it is an overreaction, but we assure you that the second you put full color in a design, it evokes visceral reactions.

In the Enlighten stage, you were showing what is plausible. You needed the audience to see your vision and believe that they can make changes you suggested. For this, you used a storyboard or a simple low-fidelity visualization.

In this stage, you will either be seeking an endorsement or projecting confidence to gain approval. The option you choose will depend on your organization's culture. Seek agreement if you suspect that people may feel slightly threatened by the new ideas or may feel as if you are interfering with their plans. If this is the case, make a conscious effort to ensure your audience knows that the ideas are a possible implementation, not a certainty. An effective way to do this is to use the pencil sketch, a low-fidelity visualization, or to add a little more depth and use black and white wireframes, which are digital representations of screens or interfaces that are typically drawn to scale. You should also continue to use couching words such as "may" and "could."

If you are in an organization that does not have ownership concerns, where you are showing somebody what is *likely*, and the feedback loop is more restricted, project confidence in your ideas by making the suggestions higher fidelity. Higher fidelity may mean that you include color, depth, and detail in your images and fewer couching words in your language. This type of visualization in product design is typically referred to as a "mockup." Mockups are a great tool used by designers to elicit feedback; in innovation, we borrow mockups as an engaging way to visualize ideas for your audience.

If you have not completed your paths in enough detail to supply your teams with the level of information they will need, you can kick off a series of research spikes to generate the details. Examples of details that you may want to include are as follows:

- Specific workflows for a step or journey
- Use cases or examples that visualize the full process and make ideas clear and tangible for an audience
- High-level understanding of how you could achieve the recommendations
- Partner recommendations and integration options that list people, companies, or technologies that provide specific services that are required for any path
- A perspective on the financial feasibility and desirability of implementing your paths.

Hold Your Meetings

You have your list of who you need to talk to. You know what you need to ask of them. And you have the materials to present to them. The next step is to set up the meetings and outreach.

Think about the way each group typically behaves and what is expected within your organization. Consider whether they prefer small group chats, group meetings, or formal presentations. Some teams send prereports to read followed by an interactive meeting. For those who are slide-inclined, prepare a slide presentation. For those who are interaction inclined, consider a professional user experience design tool for an interactive experience. For those who prefer to be visually engaged, a summary video with a vision may be most impactful. Play to the preferences of your audience so that a new format or setting does not distract from your message.

You will know your organization better than anyone else. We cannot predict the personality or behaviors of your coworkers. However, in the decades of experience this team has with leadership, we have learned that your chances of success will improve significantly if you have a premeeting with the decision makers. We do not recommend walking into a meeting in which the decision makers are deciding the fate of your project if they are hearing about it for the first time. Additionally, if there are any people in your internal relationship map who may be offended or feel threatened by your findings, you must premeet with them in a one-on-one setting to get alignment before any group meetings.

Conduct Buy-In Meetings and Ask for What You Need

When you have gotten to this step, take a moment to congratulate yourself and the team and enjoy a deep, calming breath. Then gather your energy for a roadshow! Your team will go out and present your information to many groups. But if you just go out and present without considering one more thing, you will have achieved nothing more than *training*. What you need is commitment.

Taking a page from best practices in sales, to generate commitment, you need to:

- Do your homework. (Check! You did this in the first three stages of the Compassion-Driven Innovation methodology and in building your organizational relationship map.)
- Communicate the goal. (Check! This is what you put together with your theme and in your communication strategy.)

- Pitch the solution. (Check! This is why you tell stories and use paths. Be careful here. DO NOT pitch a product; use your map from "Understanding the Challenges" to frame the discussion.)
- Predict and address objections up front. (Check! This is why you premeet with your audience.)

Now in these meetings you need to:

- Ask for the sale.
- Arrange the next steps.

Get ready to ask for the sale by formalizing what you need. State your overall goal for having the roadshow. Common overall goals include the following:

- Get approval and investment commitment of time and resources to implement some or all of a path.
- Obtain a definitive decision to continue or discontinue a project.

Once you know your overall goal for the roadshow you are about to embark on, consider your goal for each meeting. What specifically are you asking for? Determine who will be present, what you need from them, and how to request it to get what your project needs. Some specific goals may include the following:

- Assignment of people to implement suggestions
- Financial support for a project
- Agreement to generate messaging and sales models to align with the Crawl path.

When conducting the meeting, conversation or session, you can structure it to follow the sales process. Keeping in mind the audience, and your eventual request in the meeting you will: show you did your homework; communicate your goals (what you need from the org and what you need from this specific conversation); propose the solution showing how it meets the user needs; address known objections: and then make your request.

 Activate

You should close each meeting by setting up the next steps. If you achieved the goal, what will you do next together to move it forward? If you did not get commitment on your goals, what are the next steps you need to do together to move toward the goal? Are there additional considerations or research spikes? You may need to take the feedback and next steps and revisit an earlier step. This is fine. You are here to pivot *early*. Pivoting here instead of after you build your project is a win.

Why Projects Perish in This Stage

We see projects fade away or get cancelled abruptly for many reasons: Poor scoping, failure to communicate, lack of ownership, politics, culture, and so on.

If your team underestimated the cost or effort that would be required to meet the minimum acceptable solution as defined in your Crawl path, or if the cost of your Crawl proposal outweighs the benefits, prepare to have your project rejected. This means that the cost of effort to execute the project exceeds the business's appetite to move the project forward. This could be because of an actual cost-to-benefit mismatch or it could be because you fell short in communicating the business case and upside.

If you do not bring the decision makers along in your journey of innovation, you may find that no one will take on your innovation. Next time, you need to consider bringing different people into the core team to scope the theme. In this type of culture, you need to be meticulous about the amount and type of communications that are done if you want your innovation to make it to market.

Activity: Put Share into Action

- ☐ Build your internal relationship map.
- ☐ Communicate your vision and incorporate input.
- ☐ Build your presentations.
- ☐ Conduct buy-in meetings.
- ☐ Ask for what you need.

Formalize Your Innovation With a Handshake

Congratulations! You exited the Share step. You likely have approval of a path (or steps within a path) to pursue, and your next step is resourced. Now you formalize and solidify your innovation. The Compassion-Driven Innovation methodology does this with a "handshake."

In this step, you will use any committed resources from the Share step to extend the team. The activities you complete will depend on the nature of your innovation. For example, in the case of Innovation: Africa, the innovation may be completed during this step by building the journey and checklists themselves. In a case such as Gutter Tex, you may build the new processes, training, and generate high-fidelity mock-ups for a salesperson software solution. In the case of AceraEI, the innovation may be completed by delivering the full journey map along with the identified documents for each one of the 10 "Tools to Transform Schools."

Generally, you will start this step by creating working versions of the paths which have been approved. Where you cannot complete activities, you may choose to create prototypes. Then, you will conduct research spikes to resolve missing pieces or gain clarity. You may end this step when the team completes the actual implementation of your approved path. Alternatively, you may choose to set the output of the Handshake step to be high-fidelity prototypes which are input to your formal development or implementation process.

If your approved path is a series of processes, documents, marketing, and messaging, use this step to complete the activities directly. Create research spikes to determine exactly who will implement each step and how it will be implemented. For any activity that cannot be completed by your team, you will need to make sure your research spike creates enough specificity that another team can implement the idea. You can do this by creating high-resolution, detailed versions of your storyboards, perhaps resulting in workflows, requirements documents, or product designs.

If you have an approved path that requires a significant investment in development or other resources, the Handshake will manifest as artifacts

such as high-fidelity mockups, requirements documents, prototypes, and knowledge transfer. Further prepare your approved paths by working with any implementation team members to build prototypes for complex ideas. You may even wish to work with the new team while they implement the ideas for a period of time. If you have a development process in place, this is typically a great place to enter a lean or agile implementation process. If you are an organization that is large enough to have a separate implementation team, tailor your handoff to match the needs of the team that intends to implement the innovation. Just giving the documents to someone and asking them to implement the innovation will not succeed.

Care and feeding of your innovation may be required for a long period of time. We have found that sometimes the innovation we defined can take months or years to enter the development lifecycle and then reach customers. Creating detailed artifacts and traceable work will enable you to pick the content and ideas back up quickly to shepherd your innovations forward.

Example of Handshake for Innovation: Africa

For Innovation: Africa, the Handshake is the delivery of the full journey map along with the identified documents.

To complete the Handshake, the team designed the knowledge-based checklists for how to select a village. They created decision trees for how to determine the best ways to support the selected village (including options such as access to clean water or providing electricity to the school or the medical center). They then implemented the directions on how to supply the support mechanisms, including the blueprint of the water tower that is used in every water project, and installation instructions and training. Every new project will follow the journey as the right process by using the supporting documents.

As is the case in all innovation, what is created in the Handshake step will be a point-in-time representation, and lessons learned after each project can be incorporated and curated into the content as development moves forward.

Example of Handshake for Gutter Tex

As a small business with the co-owners involved in the innovation, Gutter Tex was able to move quickly through the Handshake step, which included:

- Design the website online booking systems.
- Design the ordering system back ends to enable the vision of a touchless and optimized process.
- Create new agreements and insurance requirements to allow salespersons and installation crews to go onto the homeowner property at the scheduled time with no homeowner present.
- Create salesperson training for new workflow and process.

To complete this Handshake, the team sat together and designed the new booking and ordering system. They decided on the software to use, the systems that would need to support it. They implemented new training for the sales teams and installation engineers. Gutter Tex is already well on their way to achieving their final Run path.

Example of Handshake for AceraEI

In AceraEI, the Handshake is the delivery of the full journey map along with the identified documents for each one of the 10 "Tools to Transform Schools."

To complete the Handshake step, the team documented the philosophy, curriculum, and pedagogy for the "Tools to Transform Schools "and started assessing impact to:

- Reinvent STEAM education with toolkits.
- Hold workshops with public school leaders and teachers, identifying and refining tools for adoption and creating cohorts.
- Measure school success using outcome-based dashboards.
- Complete a whole school engagement where ultimate ownership is achieved as teachers adapt the tools to meet their needs.

AceraEI is in their early stage of achieving the final Run Path.

Activity: Put Handshake into Action

☐ Extend your team to add resources for prototyping.
☐ Resolve or complete journey steps that can be completed.
☐ Create high-fidelity prototypes.
☐ Perform research spikes where needed to resolve missing pieces.
☐ Complete the Crawl path or high-fidelity prototypes with expanded teams.

Measure and Improve Your Process

Innovation must be ongoing. When you finish with one project, you may work on a new project uncovered by the Discover stage or even move onto a completely new area of research. However, you do not want to do things exactly the same way and repeat the same mistakes—after all, that is the definition of insanity, according to Einstein.

In this step, you will work as a team to objectively understand how the last project went. Your goal is to gain a mutual understanding of what happened and identify ways to improve on your next pass through. You will use these findings to expand or update the Compassion-Driven Innovation checklist in each step so that they align more closely with your direct organizational needs.

We recommend using a retrospective to formalize the Improve step, as explained in the next section.

Use a Retrospective

If every project were perfect, we would have no need for retrospectives. The innovators in our case studies are the first to say that their approach was not perfect, that they learned by trial and error. We are immensely grateful for the honor of learning their stories and sharing just a portion of their journeys with you.

Nor is the Compassion-Driven Innovation methodology perfect. We will continue to work with it, refining and adding steps when we realize what we have missed. After decades of innovation, we continually find new ways to adjust, adapt, and improve. We hope that you can use this information to move your innovation forward, and bring new compassionate, ethical solutions to solve the challenges you uncover.

Agile retrospectives are effective ways to run objective assessment meetings. This process does not allow for pointing fingers. It sets a standard of interaction, enables a review of the results, and helps determine ways to move forward effectively. You review how the project went and learn to do better using the wisdom of the team. A simple online search on "how to run an agile retrospective" will return exceptional examples of how to run your meetings, as well as links to templates and videos you can use.

We have discovered what works for our teams and share it here in case it helps you. To run an effective Compassion-Driven Innovation retrospective, you will need to perform setup activities, run the meeting, and then perform follow-up activities.

For setup, prior to your retrospective, you will assign a retrospective leader. This person will:

- **Schedule a time**, typically one hour.
    o Determine which tools will work best for the situation (video conference, in person, and so on).
    o Invite critical stakeholders and team members, keeping the number reasonable—typically under 10 attendees.
    o Set the retrospective agenda as follows:
       – Rules review
       – Shared board access
       – Generation of statements in silence
       – Grouping of statements
       – Reading of ideas and having an open discussion
       – Voting on most critical issues
       – Establishing action items.

- **Generate the shared board.** The leader will use whichever collaboration technology is available to the team. We use Miro, Easyretro.io, Teams whiteboards, or physical whiteboards with sticky notes. In the shared board, each team member must be able to create anonymous sticky notes or comments in three different areas (typically laid out as columns). You also will need the ability to move these comments or notes or group them in an order. Once the items are grouped, you will ask the team to vote on the items of highest importance. Your shared board might look like Figure 5.3.

WENT WELL	TO IMPROVE	ACTION ITEMS
Nice work on the state-of-the-art by Pat!	Forgot to include Chris up front. :(	Update Activate list with business list.
Generated four patent filings.	Missed new digital asset capabilities.	

Figure 5.3 Example of a shared board

Run the Meeting

During the meeting, the retrospective leader will read out loud the rules of engagement. These rules should honor your organization values and priorities but should at minimum include: no personal attacks or blame, keeping an open mind and dialog, and focusing on the future. You will also determine whether the outputs of the meeting will be shared and, if so, how they will be shared.

The leader then opens access to the retrospective shared board. The leader will explain to the team members that there will be a period of 5 to 10 minutes to silently generate all of the comments that they would like for the What Went Well and What We Could Improve categories. Each attendee should list one item per sticky note. List things that happened during the project. Do not solve or assign blame in the comments. Simply list your perception of what happened. The attendees will place the notes under the appropriate comment as they create them or at the end of the time period. This is up to the leader.

When the time is up, the leader will silently read each note and group notes into subcategories. This allows for the identification of duplicates and simplifies the discussion.

The leader then walks through the groups of comments. The team holds an open dialog to ensure that all team members understand what is written. The dialog does not defend or counter any writing. This process honors every perception of an experience as valid in the context of this discussion. It allows for open assessment of the circumstances. It allows space for thoughts and feelings about the circumstances. It looks at the results of the project.

Once all comments have been discussed and understood, the leader invites each team member to vote on three comments for which they would like to generate an action item. They will either physically mark on the comments (put a tick mark on a sticky note) or upvote. This will be dictated by the technology you chose. The three comments with the most tick marks will then be discussed to decide on action items.

To determine action items, all contributors may provide feedback on the comments, the surrounding circumstances, and recommendations for improvement moving forward. The leader creates notes on the action items and places them in the Action Items column. The team votes on one or more action items to implement.

Following the meeting, the leader sends notes about what was determined to be the action items and assign people to implement the actions.

Assess Success

Innovation measurement is incredibly difficult. It often takes years for innovation to make it to market. However, that does not mean that you should not at least attempt to measure your work.

Some types of measurement of success that could be attached to the innovation which was discovered include:

- Effectiveness in solving discovered challenges
- Net Promoter Scores for offerings, services, customer sentiment, or other measures that are meaningful in your area

- Paper acceptance rate
- Industry Awards
- Patents
- Internal and external reference metrics
- Open source projects
- Community engagement (for example, check-ins, code, and downloads)
- New products to market
- New companies formed
- Revenue impact.

But it is not just the outputs that should be assessed. You should take into consideration how the project went and whether you were able to achieve adoption. Consider each of the following:

- New relationships created
- Organizational buy-in
- Thought leadership.

Take time to determine what your organizational innovation performance indicators will be. Include this insight in your next project as part of your theme.

Activity: Put Improve into Action

☐ Run a retrospective meeting with your team to review what went wrong and right in the process.
☐ Add all findings to your existing checklists and processes.

Add the Missing L

We did not include *Lead* in our IDEA stages because adding the "L" relies on you and how you choose to implement the four stages of Compassion-Driven Innovation.

While translations from the ancient Roman vary, Ovid is widely credited with saying that "Dripping water hollows out stone, not through force, but through persistence." Water uses gravity to its advantage. As water gains momentum, it no longer has to follow the path of least resistance. It is an apt metaphor for creating organizational change.

No methodology is ideal. They all need to be adapted through practical application and iterative use to suit your unique environment, organization, and skill sets. How well each stage works depends on team members' intrinsic motivation to solve problems, the clarity with which the challenges are understood and documented, the invention or existence of solutions to the challenges, and your ability to generate organizational buy-in. It also depends on your ability to trust your team members, and your organizations' ability to trust you.

While *Compassion-Driven Innovation* is not designed for the lone wolf, someone in your organization has to break from tradition to lead the way. Given that you will be saving time and money and being a positive organizational force for good by using this process vs. activating an idea without using Compassion-Driven Innovation techniques, we hope this will not be a hard sell. But we understand that the longer an organization has been operating, the more likely it is to have established ways of doing things. In these environments, introducing new methodologies can feel like turning a ship that has lost power in a shallow channel.

Use an Inbound Marketing Process

If you are not familiar with inbound marketing, you will want to add it to your survival kit. Inbound marketing is a technique that attracts others to your ideas using engaging content (papers, presentations, videos, and so on) that you create.

Sharing your expertise selflessly through this content can lead like-minded people to "follow" you via internal and external social media tools and eventually even reach out to you for purposes of collaboration. You can use this process effectively with internal and external audiences to build a pool of potential contributors to future projects. When you are ready to begin a project, try discussing your topic person-to-person to gauge interest and expertise. We know it works: This is the process by which we found each other and decided to write this book together.

Introduce Change Incrementally

For most people, change is difficult; change forced upon anyone is downright tough. Rather than trying to force change all at once, we subscribe to the idea that success begets success. Consider using the Compassion-Driven Innovation methodology in a small project that you control. Prove in one project that using it can add value. Then use that project success to drive the process into another project. Building momentum through success will generate a "pull" where others start asking you how you achieved high-value results. This may feel like a long way around, but it is often easier than trying to push a methodology on people from the top down.

If you feel like you are forging a path of compassion in isolation, you may need to do more networking to find your team. You are not alone, and this path is worthwhile. Somewhere in your perimeter, a colleague is floating about on a dust speck shouting "I'm here! I'm here!"

Innovate Compassionately

In practice, we see elements of compassion-driven innovation taking off in many directions. It is grounded in the experiences of leaders like Sivan Ya'ari, Danielle Ouellette, and Courtney Dickinson. You can become more like them.

Choose compassion; dare to imagine a better world; and do not be afraid to take on challenges day by day, keeping your eyes on your North Star, and pivoting to correct your course as you learn and grow in your quest to "make good better."

Appendix A

The Checklists

Include Checklist

- ☐ Identify your project.
- ☐ Form your team.
    - ☐ Consider the initial problem the project is trying to solve.
    - ☐ Decide on the innovation type.
    - ☐ Determine discipline areas and skills of interest.
    - ☐ Build the team.
- ☐ Learn what exists.
    - ☐ Craft your theme(s) as a team.
    - ☐ Perform state-of-the-art research.
- ☐ Assert what you know.
    - ☐ Identify proto-personas.
    - ☐ Create proto-maps.
    - ☐ Write what you know.

Discover Checklist

- ☐ Validate your understanding.
  - ☐ Develop nonleading questions.
  - ☐ Script your interviews.
  - ☐ Conduct outreach.
- ☐ Analyze the data.
  - ☐ Generate new maps.
  - ☐ Revisit personas to do a bottoms-up validation of your findings.
- ☐ Understand the challenges.
  - ☐ Create challenge maps.
  - ☐ Spin out challenges and projects.

Enlighten Checklist

- ☐ Solve the challenges.
  - ☐ Create Run, Crawl, and Walk paths.
    - ☐ Conduct research spikes.
    - ☐ Create the journey and requirements document outputs.
  - ☐ Protect value (patents and so on).
  - ☐ Assess the ethical implications of your paths.
- ☐ Storytell.
  - ☐ Draw the storyboards.
  - ☐ Script the storyboards.
- ☐ Test the story.
  - ☐ Recruit interviews.
  - ☐ Run the feedback interviews.
  - ☐ Analyze the results.

Activate Checklist

- ☐ Prepare to share your innovation.
  - ☐ Build your internal relationship map.
  - ☐ Communicate your vision and incorporate input.
  - ☐ Build your presentations.
  - ☐ Conduct buy-in meetings.
  - ☐ Ask for what you need.
- ☐ Formalize your innovation with a handshake.
  - ☐ Extend your team to add resources for prototyping.
  - ☐ Resolve or complete journey steps that can be completed.
  - ☐ Create high-fidelity prototypes.
  - ☐ Perform research spikes where needed to resolve missing pieces.
  - ☐ Complete the Crawl path or high-fidelity prototypes with expanded teams.
- ☐ Measure and improve your process.
  - ☐ Run a retrospective meeting with your team to review what went wrong and right in the process.
  - ☐ Add all findings to your existing checklists and processes.

About the Authors

Nicole Reineke is a Senior Distinguished Engineer and innovation leader in the office of the CTO at Dell Technologies. She has founded and led high-tech companies, driving innovation into products and services while filing more than 70 patents. She practices and hones the transformative process of Compassion-Driven Innovation at work and with small businesses and nonprofits. She has published extensively on topics such as data management, operations, and business resiliency. Her research on innovation has been presented at the Berkeley Innovation Forum. She holds an MBA in Information Technology and has completed post graduate work in User Experience Design.

Debra Slapak is a Senior Marketing Consultant at Dell Technologies. She has built a career centered on science and technology as a marketing and sales executive, university educator, and registered nurse and case manager. She has held product management, strategic marketing, business development, research, communications, and creative roles across two Fortune 50 companies. She holds a degree in applied science and an MEd in English, as well as a postgraduate certification in strategic marketing. She devotes time to helping nonprofits create strategic marketing plans and communications with a focus on compassion for their stakeholders.

Hanna Yehuda is a Senior Distinguished Engineer and Experience Strategist in the office of the CTO at Dell Technologies. She currently leads projects at the intersection between experience design and business strategy. With over 20 years of experience, Hanna has consulted to emphasize the strategic value of experience in research and design of products and services in startups and enterprises, while filing and holding more than 50 U.S. patents. She practices the Compassion-Driven Innovation methodology at work, helping nonprofits and when mentoring new experience design practitioners. She has a BS in computer science and an MS in Human Factors in Information Design.

Index

OTHER TITLES IN THE SERVICE SYSTEMS AND INNOVATIONS IN BUSINESS AND SOCIETY COLLECTION

Jim Spohrer, IBM, and Haluk Demirkan, University of Washington, Tacoma, Editors

- *Adoption and Adaption in Digital Business* by Bhuvan Unhelkar
- *Customer Value Starvation Can Kill* by Walter Vieira
- *Build Better Brains* by Martina Muttke
- *ATOM, Second Edition* by Kartik Gada
- *Designing Service Processes to Unlock Value, Third Edition* by Joy M. Field
- *Disruptive Innovation and Digital Transformation* by Marguerite L. Johnson
- *Service Excellence in Organizations, Volume II* by Fiona Urquhart
- *Service Excellence in Organizations, Volume I* by Fiona Urquhart
- *Obtaining Value from Big Data for Service Systems, Volume II* by Stephen H. Kaisler, Armour, and J. Alberto Espinosa
- *Obtaining Value from Big Data for Service Systems, Volume I* by Stephen H. Kaisler, Armour, and J. Alberto Espinosa

Concise and Applied Business Books

The Collection listed above is one of 30 business subject collections that Business Expert Press has grown to make BEP a premiere publisher of print and digital books. Our concise and applied books are for...

- Professionals and Practitioners
- Faculty who adopt our books for courses
- Librarians who know that BEP's Digital Libraries are a unique way to offer students ebooks to download, not restricted with any digital rights management
- Executive Training Course Leaders
- Business Seminar Organizers

Business Expert Press books are for anyone who needs to dig deeper on business ideas, goals, and solutions to everyday problems. Whether one print book, one ebook, or buying a digital library of 110 ebooks, we remain the affordable and smart way to be business smart. For more information, please visit www.businessexpertpress.com, or contact sales@businessexpertpress.com.

CPSIA information can be obtained
at www.ICGtesting.com
Printed in the USA
BVHW041219080122
625637BV00005B/60